ROBERT WHITE

INCLUDES ACCESS TO THE **KHQ** STUDY APP

I AM A MAN

FREE BOBBY

BLACK POWER

THE *OR ELSE!* FACTOR

A LEGACY OF AFRICAN AMERICAN RESISTANCE AND A BLUEPRINT FOR COMMUNITY ORGANIZING

THE *OR ELSE!* FACTOR

A LEGACY OF AFRICAN AMERICAN RESISTANCE AND
A BLUEPRINT FOR COMMUNITY ORGANIZING

Robert O. White II

Kendall Hunt
publishing company

Cover image © Shutterstock.com

Kendall Hunt
publishing company

www.kendallhunt.com
Send all inquiries to:
4050 Westmark Drive
Dubuque, IA 52004-1840

Copyright © 2021 by Kendall Hunt Publishing Company

PAK ISBN: 978-1-7924-9720-9
Text ISBN: 978-1-7924-9719-3

All rights reserved. No part of this publication may be reproduced, stored in a retrieval system, or transmitted, in any form or by any means, electronic, mechanical, photocopying, recording, or otherwise, without the prior written permission of the copyright owner.

Published in the United States of America

Contents

About the Author v

About This Book vii

Forever Forward ix

Introduction xxiii

CHAPTER 1: What Do We Want? 1

CHAPTER 2: The Art of Casual Complaint 11

CHAPTER 3: By Power, We Get Things Done 23

CHAPTER 4: Profiles of Community Organization 31

CHAPTER 5: The Games People Play 37

Bibliography 43

About the Author

Dr. Robert O. White II is an educator, legal analyst and pastor with over 27 years of professional experience. He has taught in higher education for over twenty years and has accumulated a wealth of experience over the course of his professional career. He served as in-house legal counsel for the Alabama Education Association and interim Director of Voter Registration and Elections for the Secretary of State's Office. He has served as government liaison and lobbyist for government and professional development agencies as well. He is co-founder of the first registered African American alternative energy company in the state of Alabama: Quail Energy. He has produced several radio talk shows, contributed to many scholarly works, published six books, co-authored two books and is currently finishing three more on the topic of civil rights and spirituality. He is also working on a video documentary that chronicles the civil rights history associated with the Black Belt of Alabama. He has given scores of scholarly presentations and has served on many academic and community committees. He has served as program chairman for the Montgomery Improvement Association and he is a member of the NAACP. He has served as student advisor to the Alabama State University Student Government Association and several other committees on campus. He has been secretary for the Alabama Political Science Association and a former board member for the Center for the Study of Civil Rights and African American Culture. He has served in leadership capacities in the AFL-CIO, the American Federation of Teachers, the National Education Association, the Alabama Education Association and is currently the president of the Alabama State University Education Association. He serves on the National Education Association Editorial Board and has assisted in union organizing throughout the country. He has helped several community organizations and his specialty is encouraging and advising young people. He is currently along with his wife pastoring the Montgomery City of Refuge. He has been a member of the distinguished faculty of Alabama State University for over 26 years and also serves as adjunct instructor for other local colleges. He is married to Nichelle White (25 years) and has one daughter (Charity) and many students that he has mentored over the years. His passion and conviction is raising the consciousness of today's young people and winning the lost for Jesus Christ His theme for organizing is: "Aint gone let no body push us around!" There is only one form of justice and that is God's justice and there is only one salvation and that is the grace of Jesus Christ.

About This Book

With the passing of C.T. Vivian, John Lewis, Gloria Richardson, Robert Moses and a whole generation of anticolonial stalwarts, we, as a black whole, are called not to just mourn, but to understand, embrace and reproduce their legacies as organizational achievements which live or die based on our capacity and willingness to reproduce and build on them. Throughout the post-Civil Rights and Black Power era, there's been a struggle for historical memory that's been based more on individual heroism and courage than on the institutional and political aspirations for the organized collective that their political and institutional goals served. This oversight halves our engagement with their contributions to history and it deliberately undermines their relevance to new generations of organizers that already exist, and that have not yet been made.

Just like the abolitionist movement and revolutionary activities of the slaves throughout the diaspora threatened the very global economic system that gave rise to slavery and colonialism, the civil rights movement threatened to turn the known world upside because so much of the issues centered on race. We have identified that the distinguishing factor in the success or failure of social movements in America and the world over is predicated on the use of good threats, or the 'Or Else Factor!' "Either you give us our rights, or else!" This book is dedicated to the foot soldiers who risked life and limb to raise the consciousness of the world regarding the role that suffering plays in the quest for freedom and truth. Although many have fallen asleep, there remains a remnant of freedom fighters who have maintained a revolutionary vigil in hopes that somehow the fire of their times can be rekindled. While some names are preeminent in civil rights discussions, the more research we do and the more interaction that we have with those in the movement, the more sure we become in concluding that there is not any one person whose name should be synonymous with a movement that involved so many courageous people; many of who remain unknown even unto this day. We celebrate those who have passed on like John Hulett, Fannie Lou Hammer, Bruce Boynton and those who remain like Annie Pearl Avery and Mukassa Dada "Willie Ricks." Those in the civil rights movement, like those slaves and freedmen who preceded them, were the first to say "Give us our freedom or else" in various ways, and the Black Belt of Alabama was ground zero for what would become the birth of the modern civil rights movement. The revolutionary spirit of the movement can be seen in many local grassroots personalities from around the country, the islands and the west coast of Africa. Slaves like Nat Turner and Denmark Vessey, islanders like Nutty Bookman and Paul Bogle did the same thing by using any and all means available to secure their freedom. It was Denmark Vessey's church that was attacked by Dylann Roof because even in his derangement, he knew that it was a strategic location to black revolutionary thought. Specifically, the Black Belt of Alabama was the central meeting place of many eagles from around the world at the turn of the civil rights movement and even to this day, thousands of people congregate every year to commemorate the events that took place there. Specifically, we consider U.S. Highway 80, which runs from one end of the southeastern United States to the other, a corridor for civil rights because it links the events which took place in Alabama's Black Belt to the rest of the United States south and the world. The Or Else Factor is dedicated to all of the freedom fighters, black and white, who made a science out of standing up to oppression.

Forever Forward

The Return of Jim Crow Fo Sho!

The Jim Crow era began with a nail biter presidential election between Rutherford B. Hayes and Samuel J. Tilden. The agreement struck between one of the candidates Rutherford B. Hayes, known as the Compromise of 1787, not only promised to return political power into the hands of the former slave owners, but it served as a continuance of previous compromises like the 3/5ths Compromise and the Fugitive Slave Act, where the Negro or slave was sold out for political gain. The supporters of the Jim Crow culture instituted a system worse than slavery because it was then that the colored person had no rights that whites were bound to respect. Specifically, the notable political gains that freedmen did obtain were violently and ruthlessly taken away. Yet this divesture of human dignity was not only done in America, the world was witnessing the emergence of a colonial system which put light against dark, foreigner against indigenous, race and gender to the point that people in their own land had to have passports to move about. In America, Jim Crow imposed a vicious form of segregation by limiting the education, opportunity and mobility of black people; something Martin Luther King noted remained even after the passage of the Voting Rights Act. Despite the many lawsuits and resolutions passed, one court case that was actually dismissed did more to strike a dagger in the Alabama Jim Crow system than any other, and it was done by someone who had been formerly incarcerated in the Alabama Department of Corrections. Kenneth Glasgow filed suit in federal court to raise the consciousness of the nation's grassroots effort. Rev. Kenneth Glasgow and The Ordinary People's Society are responsible for one of the most significant victories in the modern civil rights movement. Through the efforts of he and his band of advocates, which included the adoption of new voting policy, the clarification of vague constitutional questions which restricted the rights of incarcerated persons, the filing of the federal lawsuit styled Glasgow v. Allen and the establishment of voting rights reform legislation in the state, Alabama seemed ready to move forward in making the electoral process a mechanism of change. At the center of the controversy was the qualification of felony convictions that involved moral turpitude; which was determined to be too vague a term to justify the nullification of voting rights. During the course of the new voting rights movement, the question was asked which gave rise to the major concern over the use of critical race theory by some today: "What is the impact of the Jim Crow system on the gross national product of Alabama and How much did the long lasting system of Jim Crow cost the citizens of Alabama?" The effort of Glasgow and TOPS revealed that thousands of people had been wrongfully denied the right to vote for decades without recourse and both sides of the political isles had done nothing to address it. From this we know that established political power does not want new voters, poor voters or those disfranchised to vote. It is the possibility of hope coming to the hopeless and power for the powerless that stirs efforts to take away the voting rights from as many people as possible. When we ask these critical questions, the illogical and unreasonable aspect of race prejudices emerge because the short answer would be that we would have a much better handle on the negative social indicators had Jim Crow politics not been employed to handicap a significant population of Alabama voters and that black leadership is as much to blame for sustained political shortcomings as the white leadership; both being sustained by the same system.

Amelia Boynton, the mother of the Voting Rights Movement, and the Rev Kenneth Glasgow its Seventh Son, did much to advance the cause of voting rights in their respective times, yet the forces at work to minimize the impact of local political organizers is a science that is seldom studied. As the reader might know, all politics are local and nothing was as polarizing in Alabama politics as the election of President Barack Obama. While the fallout from the possibility of an African American president was predictable, especially to some of Alabama's old school black politicians, the impact that an Obama presidency would have on local politics was not thoroughly thought out, nor were many white Alabamians accepting of the fact that a Negro was in the White House and after the Obama election, the fear mongers went to work to unify the white vote in Alabama and they were successful. Just like the backlash from Booker T. Washington's visit to the White House in his day was considered a breach of Jim Crow etiquette, The Obama administration served as a rallying cry for enraged southerners to Rise Again and the Confederate flags took on a new symbolism—more reaching than in the past! After all, at the time of the Obama presidency, the State had no statewide black elected officials, no black judges serving on the Alabama Court of Criminal or Civil Appeals and no black State Supreme Court judges. The state also has no black constitutionally elected officials. While the Shelby County v. Holder case, which was a matter of local election law implementation that gutted the Voting Rights Act, the state's legislature passed strict voter ID laws claiming wide spread fraud; which could have been addressed by the Voting Rights Act had it been amended with a new coverage formula. How can there be enough evidence of voter fraud to warrant a voter ID bill but not enough to warrant a renewal or strengthening of the Voting Rights Act? Also had the Voting Rights Act been allowed to stand, the ex-post facto contestation of the election results by the supporters of the Trump campaign that were banned by laches could have been challenged under the preclearance provision, but who thinks of those things? "What scared a lot of people about President Obama, especially those on the paranoid right, was not the fact that he was a Constitutional Law professor or that he was a U.S. Senator or his imaginary lack of citizenship or even that he was black—although the color line in American society is a decisive factor in American social policy." No, their main fear was that he was a "community organizer" who had worked his way up to the office from the obscurity of grassroots efforts. To some, President Obama was a nightmare. To those steeped in tradition on both sides of the aisle, any one person, even a trouble maker, can make it to the most powerful seat in the world. I don't think we have studied the traditional role that grassroots community organizers have played in the threat posed to established governmental control of common people at the local level. The election of President Obama proved to the thousands of community organizers who felt powerless that they did not have to come from a rich family or political legacy to obtain political power. Yet having a strategic understanding of underpinning issues is critical in addressing sustained poverty, violence and disfranchisement; all of which are done away with through revolutionary means and not just by mere reformation. Hidden within the pathos of American social order is the overwhelming possibility that poor people could take over the country. The rise of the poor to take control of the country is the single biggest fear in the pathology of American politics and not enough has been done to analyze the fears to some of the rise of an energized and electrified poor revolutionary constituency the fears of which lay deep in the pathos of American social order.

Somewhere between Ayn Rand's *Atlas Shrugged*, W.E.B. Du Bois' *Souls of Black Folk* and Saul Alinsky's *Rules for Radicles* is a paradigm from which African Americans can organize to better their conditions from within the western concept of freedom and liberty. However, for building a revolutionary personality, the need to study African American revolutionary thinkers emerges. While it has been assumed that black folks in making demands for equality are simply imitating others, it is clear that black people want what others want; that is to be free to be themselves without fear of being retaliated against from the mob. Black Lives Matter and the (take a knee) movement showed that corporate dollars override public sentiment and the Or Else Factor at least gets the attention of those businesses whose profits depend on an accurate understanding of public consumer culture. These movements and other local groups like the Communities Not Prisons movement in Alabama have proven that making threats of boycotts, press conferences and demonstrations gets the attention of those with the power and these corporate boards are willing to make changes for the better.

The death of George Floyd ignited a sentiment that continues to grow in America and with each death at the hands of dirty cops, the rising tide of black resistance grows higher. The local protestors and demonstrators whether they know it or not, are fighting a system much bigger than their local government but if local political power can be dismantled, the global system of colonialism is doomed. When the students at Auburn University, Alabama State University and the members of Communities not Prisons confronted national corporations for their proposed support of the Gov. Key Ivey's plan to build three private prisons in Alabama, they by passed the state government and went right to the streets; protesting directly in front of the corporate headquarters of the banks and holding companies until they were asked into a meeting where the decision was made by corporate executives to abandon the project. With no funding, the far reaching and over extended plan to build three mega prisons was foiled. Local activists did what the state legislators could not do; that is influence the real power players that the plan was a violation of public interest. The grass roots organizers said: "Either you decline to fund these modern day plantations OR ELSE!"

Or Else can be used anywhere those seeking change are congregated. Because there is little or no incentive for whites to patronize blacks, the Or Else factor serves to threaten the profit margin of an already exploitative and dependent relationship. The global system of colonialism is supported by the fact that people of color possess the resources and the European nations pilfer it. As seen by the Haitian Revolution or the Ghanian revolution any disruption of this exploitative relationship spells economic catastrophe for the colonies.

The Or Else *Resistance* to colonialism is a critical aspect of the African American experience since the inception of the dreadful slave trade. The slave in the south and the disfranchised free Negro in the north had as advocates both Frederick Douglass and Martin Delany. The writing(s) of these two men and others makes the objective of building self-determinative measures easy because they and others believed there to be no difference between enslaved people in the south and disfranchised colored people in the north. After slavery, the freeman had Booker T. Washington, W.E.B. Du Bois and Carter G. Woodson, to name a few. Afterwards we had Martin Luther King, Marcus Garvey, Hon. Elijah Muhammed, Noble Drew Ali and Malcolm X. However, what all these people had in common was that they embraced reading as a means of embracing revolutionary realities. Anybody poised to organize people to confront injustice and statism must be a vociferous reader. I always say in my classes: "You can't lead if you don't read." The issue with the condition of African Americans is not violence, racism or lack of education. Instead, the questions of our time involve the ability to organize around realities and logical principles and not so much from emotion, religious dogma and mutual frustration. The vote was granted to the freeman after the civil war and freedmen throughout the south were elected to office by their own electorate who was no better off than those free in the North. After a brief period of political presence, the violence of the Jim Crow period, which commenced after the election of 1878, would erase almost all political power of Negroes in the south. It would not be until 1965 and the efforts of the civil rights movement in Selma, Alabama that the tide would begin a slight turn. While slavery ended in 1865, it would take 100 years for there to be serious protections offered to black voters. To blame slavery alone on the current social condition of African Americans is to totally neglect the role that resistance efforts play in the liberation of a people and liberation is something only a people can do for themselves. Liberation is not given by the oppressor but it is secured by the oppressed when they confront the source of their oppression. However, it is knowledge of the facts that gives an organizer the courage to confront the internal fears and reservations before they begin to mobilize others. Historically, this was done both by physical conflicts such as the Haitian Revolution and the Boer Wars and political advancement like the establishment of the ANC and the SNCC. Black people overwhelmingly chose non-violence because in a republic, violence is unnecessary and counterproductive. However, violence against colonialism in Africa and the Americas is as much a reality. All that is needed in a republic to do justice is honesty, logic and reason but when there is a violation of the fundamentals of liberty, the cause of organization arises. It is for this reason that white supremacy has no place in a republic because white supremacy reduces citizenship to a fallacious question of DNA and not character or merit. It is very problematic to organize around race because race, which is problematic itself as a construct, does not assume any one particular worldview or objective. So while others can organize around issues or causes, African Americans find themselves responding illogically and unreasonably to some arbitrary stimulus like the red herring known as CRT which comes from an equally illogical or unreasonable response.

If slavery and colonialism did anything, it destroyed the ability of colored people to organize themselves around the realities of their day. Instead, the entire colored world has been subject to the powers, realities, definitions and goals of Europeans. *Organization* is an intentional act by a diverse group of people to accomplish as a group what can not be accomplished by individuals. The assumption is that those seeking to organize will do so for their own benefit and interest. Yet this does not happen in the world of the African Diaspora; where people of color either indigenous or foreign find themselves being organized by others to accomplish the goals of the others. Politically speaking, organization is learned by an emerging oppressed people through the very act of liberation; a process Franz Fanon called *decolonization*. However, in the post-Obama era, things have been so sensitized that to mention colonialism, critical race theory or systemic racism is to automatically trigger defensive mechanisms from certain people in society who have no other understanding of the topics except that which has been told them by their misguided political influencers. Black people show themselves to be worthy of liberty and justice if they have organized around the realities of their life and to not get caught up in the emotional topics that incite indignation. Bobby Seale said: "The man does not have black people outnumbered but out organized" and community organization begins with the establishment of core values and principals and then the strategy works itself out.

Albert Meme identifies Colonialism as being a two party system; the oppressed and the oppressor. While the oppressed do not need the oppressor, the oppressor most certainly needs the oppressed to serve a need that is essential to the survival of the oppressor. While the slave/master relationship is exploitative in nature, the end of slavery marks an advancement in the life of the oppressed; who is not forced to live a life independent of the ones they have grown accustomed to accommodating. Colonialism involves 4 factors. The first is the occupation of the lands of colored people by foreigners who are typically European. The second is the exploitation of the resources and people of the land. The third factor is the imposition of the European values, education, language religion, and politics upon those who are colonized. Finally, the fifth factor is to impose a system that makes colonial system generational in nature which means the oppressed adults teach the younger generation of oppressed how to survive and even advance in the colonial system. Black folk in America might be familiar with slavery but the vestiges of colonialism continue to this day. Colonialism is a global event and is predicated on the geographical fact that people of dark skin typically inhabit regions of the world that are rich in natural resources. It is upon this fact that the U.S colonies were established. A lot of people reject the mention of 1619 because this date marks a starting point for the discussion of the slave trade. However, slavery began long before this date as did resistance to it on the part of the African diaspora and the indigenous people of color. Yet there are political reasons for not teaching about colonialism or anything dealing with the atrocities of the past because to do so is to continue the decolonization process which began millinea ago. Colonialism has done a serious injustice to the global population of colored people of which the local black community in America is a microcosm. Yet the point must be noticed that so many issues regarding colonialism have emerged as a result of local crisis such as the death of George Floyd. Juneteenth celebrations and intense conversations on issues like critical race theory, reparations and intersectionality come to light from local unresolved incidents which illustrates the connection between local organization and larger more expansive movements. This might be because when unrefutable evidence shows present racism, the claims of the past gain more credence. "Community organization like in the case of Trayvon Martin or Tamir Rice is a type of warfare without bloodshed. It" is a minute form of decolonization. A protestor in Atlanta, Georgia might very well carry a flag with Red Black and Green colors on it which signifies the Back to Africa Movement started by Marcus Garvey. In the case of police brutality, organizing against a corrupt police department and appealing to the United Nations for war crimes and human rights violations committed against Catholic priests and nuns in Central America are the same act and involve the same parties.

Every nation in the western world, including Europe and the United States, first fought a civil war from within before spreading their colonial ambition. Yet for people of color, every American holiday that celebrates some victory on the battlefield serves as an absurdity and contradiction to black people's experience because every war that has been fought by Americans came at a time when America was as brutal toward African Americans as toward their foreign enemies. This is also true for other races like the Italians who celebrate Columbus Day not in commemoration of Christopher Columbus' so-called discovery but in commemoration of

11 Italians who were lynched in New Orleans in 1891. We will not discuss the epic battles between the peoples of Europe which would eventually lead to their amalgamation into the European Union. However, many black people, who organize locally do so with full understanding of the international reality of race prejudice and discrimination. Yet Kwame Ture noted that it is black people in America that wear the image of the continent of Africa on their shirts, hats and around their necks. Yet the concept of race remains an illusionary concept. Because *white* as a social construct is mythical, unscientific and illogical, and has absorbed the adverse nationalities of Europe into a false social aggregate in America, white becomes equivalent to American, Western and Christian.

While slavery was bewildering and disorientating to African people on both continents, black people had an understanding of how to emerge from slavery but forgot it by accepting the education, history and religious perspective of others instead of developing their own God given self-determinative agenda from their own experience. This process of colonization was fought against with more zeal in Africa than in America. In Africa for example, the Sharpville Rebellion, led by Robert Sobukwe or the Soweto Uprising of students against colonial education which led to the death of Hector Pieterson in 1976, are examples of local efforts to make demands of the Europeans that they should not have to make on their own land. When a people free themselves through speech which leads to a violent confrontation in protecting that speech from their oppressor, that freedom comes from a struggle from within as well as without. Yet it is the unwillingness of the oppressor to render to the oppressed that which is due them that makes violence inevitable. During this time, or armed conflict, the values and principles for nation building emerge. For example, the rebellion of the colonies against the British was gruesome and obscene at first but now it is celebrated so has been the case of armed revolutions that African people have had against their colonial masters. Yet the difference is that these victories remain outside the consciousness of black people worldwide which think that the only form of resistance that they have historically created was the singing of "we shall overcome" and the mobilization of mass meetings. Seldom is attention paid to the strategies employed by Africans and African Americans at the local level to secure for themselves rights due them. Just as there were movements to remove the Confederate flags atop some of the nation's state capitals and to topple confederate monuments in American cities, Africans were removing statutes of Gandhi and Cecil John Rhodes because of their negative associations with colonialism.

Frederick Douglass was incensed when he was asked to deliver a Fourth of July speech considering that at the time of American independence, African people were enslaved. Douglass in his narrative stated that the master instituted holidays to teach the slaves how to mismanage their freedom, time and what little money they were allowed to earn. The rationale for instituting holidays was that it if the slaves were inebriated with liquor and leisure that they would forget that they were slaves nor would they use such time to plan their escape or revolt. in the case of black folks in America and colored people abroad, history has been written by others to make their freedom look like it was an act of a benevolent master and not the work of their own hands. The absurdity of racism in America is also seen if the slaves had rose up and fought for their freedom like some did, the purpose or cause of the civil war would not be an issue for us today! There was a reason why the Union army did not want to arm its black people. The reason is simple; because they might take matters into their own hands like some thought they would do having been inspired by the Haitian Revolution. After the war, the colored troops were disarmed and suffered greatly from organized mobs of whites who remained armed and vengeful against the freedmen.

Answering The Critical Theory of Race

For oppressed people, the Or Else Factor is a threat, a demand that is made against a local power structure. "Either you pave our streets, increase police presence or end the blockade in Cuba or else!" However to make threats, a community organization must have something of value that it can withhold or exert that exploits the weaknesses of the powers that be. The boycotts in Montgomery and Tuskegee like other forms of protest and selective buying that took place in the past sought to strike the white power structure in the pocket book. The people of Montgomery and Tuskegee said: "Treat us better or we will not use the buses, we will not come to work...we will only purchase from ourselves." Community organizing involves harnessing the "or else" power of local people to get what they want from the local government. "Or else" is as intellectual as it is physical and requires an understanding of the strengths and weaknesses of the ruling group. To the southern system a disruption of the southern way of life was enough to send the region into chaos. However, it must be noted that the "Or Else" in Montgomery and Selma was not a motivating factor in getting white people to change their ways. In fact, as black resistance intensified, so did white aggression. Let it be known that white people were prepared to do whatever it took to maintain social order. White people neither cattered to or caved into black people's demands. That is why the courts were the only solution and even then, it took multiple court consent decrees and multiple actions to put an end to the Jim Crow policies; some which remain in a de-facto form to this day; especially when it comes to housing. When it comes to race, whites did not recognize the law or the authority of federal authority and even at the local level mayors or governors would dare not intervene in the actions of the white mob. Race plays a significant factor in the making of the Or Else factor because race or the colorline has been the dividing line in American social order.

Community organizers seeking to be impactful must first accept that they are up against a ruling group which tries to control the day to day lives of the people; which involves the control of directions of public debate and discussion. Critical Race Theory (CRT) is an important topic for discussion because it demands that fundamental questions regarding the amount of racism and discrimination in one place be defined in qualitative and quantitative terms. An examination of the testimony offered in various discrimination law suits like that of Browder v. Gayle reveal that many of the apprehensions about the post civil rights litigation consent decrees which called for a dismantling of the Jim Crow system would lead to civil unrest and chaos. This is because race and the Jim Crow system was the underlying aspect of American society. CRT evaluates all factors including black leadership which may have not recognized critical aspects of African American existence. Yet when forces oppose it being discussed in an academic setting, it is purely because the very discussion brings to light things hidden from common view; the very factors that would make organization necessary. A critical analyzes of the African American condition and the relationship of black folks in America to other colored people of the world would reveal a set of factors from which a model of self-determination could be built. It is not an opinion or theory that race plays a major role in Americna society but it was from the mouth of the defendents in the Browder v. Gayle case and the words of Montgomery's Mayor alone which stated it. A review of the congressional records on the debates on slavery and later civil rights and desegregation reveal that if slavery or Jim Crow ended, so would American society as they knew it.

Community organizing is a matter of responsibility and when a people liberate themselves they become responsible for themselves. In the Gospels, Jesus confronted a man who laid at the pool of Bethesda for 38 years, yet when Jesus questioned him about being made whole, is answer was yes! However, when the man's infirmities were removed, so were his excuses! He was now free to fail on his own power. What message has been preached or lessons have been taught that defines just how much responsibility has been left to black people to take care of themselves? The answer to this question is critical and to some, it becomes scary when the poor answer the question by saying: "It is our responsibility to build for ourselves a future, forget the government! " In a strict sense, a community organizes to free itself from colonial government not entangle itself with it! Jim Crow was a local form of oppression that was supported by state police and federal troops. However in most instances, while state and federal law enforcement mobilized, local mayors and their police chiefs remained in control of joint law enforcement details. These forces violated the rights of people in their occupation of mostly urban areas and enforced totalitarian forms of occupation when black people took to the streets.

The African American literary tradition resembles that of the African literary tradition in many ways, but its most familiar aspect is the emphasis on self-examination and self-analysis. By so doing, the reality of the division of responsibility between the individual and the group is understood. A major aspect of early African American revolutionary and protest literature involves the definition of self-determination and responsibility. Is it a mayor's responsibility to look after the people, protect black folks and educate black folks or is it their own responsibility to do for self? There is a term called *Crow Jimism* which is applicable at this juncture. At the mid century, the government began to look into the experience of the colored people and various sympathies were created as well. Some prominent voices among the political left was to look at the black community as a charity case; a field of philanthropy. This colonialist mindset was paternal in nature and its assumption was that black people should be protected and advocated for because they were not capable of taking care of themselves or defending themselves. Despite the billions of dollars that have been spent in the nation's black communities in the area of social programs, the problems of the black belt remain because they remain improperly understood! Unfortunately, those voices who focused on self-determination have not been studied or have had their work compromised or minimized by those seeking to keep the black community in a state of dependency. At the center of the black revolutionary efforts regardless of time or place was the need to have a political education; something that is not taught in a typical school curriculum. Normally decolonization, revolution or a liberation movement come from political parties which have hashed out clearly defined principles. These parties heavily immersed themselves in the teachings of intellectuals of all races. Instead, some like Thomas Sowell and Harold Cruise believed the problem with black people is the black intellectuals who despite their books and posturing, have not built a proper organizational model from within the black community. In other words, rather than organizing themselves, black leaders have allowed others to organize them using theories and ideas that are against the best interest of black people. In the absence of clear margins of responsibility owed by black people to themselves, organization at any level is difficult.

One Must Respect Power

Power is a major theme of early African American literature. For example, Frederick Douglass define the peculiarity of power within a western social construct. Power according to Douglas gives up nothing without demand. Douglass discovered early in his life that the white man's power to enslave the black man was based on the ability of the white man to prevent the education of the black man. The Richard Wright, Malcolm

X, Kwame Ture, Martin Luther King, Kwame Nkrumah, Steve Biko and others expounded upon the necessity of obtaining power. I like the definition of power that I first learned as a young man from the labor unions; that power is the ability to promote, pursue and protect one's own self-interest and politics is the methods that are used to accomplish this task. A people without power is left vulnerable and subject to the benevolence of others and African Americans seem to be subject to forces they did not create and required to respond to circumstances they did not start . Malcom X said in his speech *Prospects For Freedom* "real power comes from conviction", and power is the underlying factor in the self-determination of any people. Malcom X was drawing a comparison between the struggles of African people on the continent and that of the struggle of other oppressed people in China. Malcom X was identifying the role scientific advances play in the liberation struggle and that only an oppressed people can save themselves by obtaining power for themselves. Hubert Harrison said that the Negro must master the subjects of chemistry and engineering which were the same subjects in which Europeans majored in which helped them subdue the world. In his speech at Morgan State University, Stokely Carmichael, also known as "Kwame Ture," defined *power* as the ability to define one's self and W.E.B. DuBois agreed that *beauty* is the main object of the power of definition. So to say "black power" like "Mukassa Dada" Willie Ricks does or to say "black is beautiful" is revolutionary and powerful. If something is beautiful then it is precious and a thing worth dying for. It is a trick of the enemy to make oppressed people think that they have nothing worth dying for!

The Role of Whites in the Black Cause

I had the chance of having a celebrity in my class not as visitor but as a student. Mrs. Jeane Graetz enrolled at Alabama State University and graduated in honors. It was one thing to have her in my class but it's another thing for history to take a seat. Her favorite personality was Marcus Garvey and her greatest regret was that she had not heard of him sooner! What if she and others who participated in the non-violent civil rights movement had been more familiar with the words of Marcus Garvey perhaps their objectives would have been a little more directed toward black nation building than merely social interaction. The late Bob and Jeane Graetz were called into the Montgomery Bus Boycott. They were a white Lutheran Pastor and Wife who came to Montgomery to pastor an all black church. Yet Pastor Graetz after arriving in Montgomery, joined the movement as an assistant to Martin Luther King. His house was bombed twice and he and his family received numerous threats from the whites. The question of white involvement in black liberation dates back to the abolition movement during slavery. While the country was mixed about whether to maintain slavery, free or admit the slaves, it became clear that not all abolitionists were for the inclusion of the slaves into American society. Some wanted the best and brightest of the Negro race shipped back to Africa while others offered other more convenient solution. During Reconstruction, white philanthropists served a critical role in the building of Negro schools. Even during the civil rights movement, the question was a divisive one; especially as black liberation organizations expanded their scope beyond the local struggle. It had been long settled with the Student Non-Violent Coordinating Committee (SNCC) in Greensboro, Mississippi that whites coming to the rescue of impoverished and oppressed blacks in the south was not a workable means to the ends of freedom. The young people under the guidance of Ella Baker and then Fannie Lou Hamer sought to deliberately organize young blacks in the Black Belt for the purpose of taking matters into their own hands through political activity. For some, this was a scary thing, for blacks to organize without the permission and oversight of white people! The fear of organizing Negroes goes back to the anxieties associated with slave revolts on plantations and the slave codes enacted to regulate the slave's activity and extends into the Jim Crow period which by law limited to the movements, congregations and associations of Negroes. To some members of SNCC, well-meaning whites could serve the cause of black power by being ambassadors to their community and not within the ranks of SNCC. Other major issues which made the expulsion of whites more inevitable were when the civil rights and black nationalist movements came out against the Vietnam War and the Arab-Israeli conflict; the latter being an accelerant for competing nationalisms between blacks and Jews in America that seemed to be reluctant to accept each other. Also, within the Jewish community personalities like Norman Podhoretz (My Negro Problem and Ours) objected to the role that black nationalist organizations played in the push for civil rights. Whether civil rights or black liberation organizations were spiritual or not, they all possessed a similar assessment of western culture: that America's fundamental weakness is the contradiction between America's boast of freedom and its actions when it comes to race. This means that whenever someone wants power, all they have to do is play the *race card* because it works! In fact, the same culture of denial, dismissal and dissidence that facilitated 400 years of slavery allows for injustice to linger and fester unchecked to this day despite its wide publication on social media. Even today, the Republicans are showing their hand; that they can only win elections when the masses of black people do not or cannot vote. They want to overturn elections, throw election results out and make the selection of the President a legislative or judicial act and not an act of the people or the Electoral College. This is a classic example of a democratic coup d'etat or mob rule. It is clear by the mad dash to overturn the election that local community organizing is at the heart of the Democratic victory and Republican defeat.

The objective of the civil rights movement was for black people and all people to be treated equal to white people. Affirmative action was not an idea of the civil rights movement nor was other forms of preference, special and exceptional treatment. Instead, black people marched, protested and boycotted to be equal, normal and to be left alone; to be left to their own ideas and logic, African Americans wanted to be left to the merits of their own ideas. It was often stated by Attorney Fred Gray, lawyer to Martin Luther King, Rosa Parks and other civil rights leaders that his intention in drafting integration policy throughout the various desegregation consent decrees in which he was involved was not so that black people would be treated special but because integration makes targeting black people that much harder, though not impossible. Yet racism has denied objectivity in our society and without organizing around an Or Else Factor all oppressed people, all that one can do is wait and hope that the system of oppression subsides or becomes sympathetic to their plight while denying the past.

However it might seem someone what over reaching to ask others to do for you those things that only one can do for his or herself.

What Did the Slaves Say?

The slaves were the experts on slavery. When they wrote, they provide a perspective that many writers of the period omit. The slaves either on the Island or the Americas always resisted their condition and their fights on the islands of the Caribbean were centralized battles. These local battles were complex to say the least yet the Europeans used diversions and superficial divisions to keep the Africans at bay. The reason why slavery lasted as long as it did, from a revolutionary standpoint was the fact that there was no common vision for the future and the various factions on the islands often times divided by skin complexion were always promised some sort of privilege in return for loyalty. Yet whatever privilege offered only served as a new form of enslavement. The slaves, maroons and mulattoes were promised opportunities but never equality. It is an observation of efforts like those on the islands of Jamaica and Haiti that are relevant to the struggle of African Americans now; that a slave will tolerate slavery, but a man will not tolerate disrespect. Once, a person discovers that they are equal to their oppressor, they will not tolerate their oppressor any longer, even if that oppressor has advantages over them. The leap from slavery to freedom is not as broad as bridging the gulf between second class citizenship and outright equality; the later is secured in blood because the oppressed in the latter cause views the absurdity of their oppressors rule and a slave does not. A slave will accept a white Jesus and all the pathology that comes with it, but when the slave learns what the master knows, he or she is equal and will destroy all the idols of his or her enslavement. It is at the point of equality that the former slave can say to his former oppressor: "cease to hinder me, or else!"

Reading is the event that marks the transformation from slavery to freedom and the application of that knowledge accelerates the progress from inferiority to equality. It is the acquisition of the fruits of that knowledge, be it in the form of property and profession, that marks the movement from childhood to manhood. The slave knew little of manhood, partly because those around him—namely his oppressors—were children themselves. Because the slaves were dealing with a very immature and primitive environment on the slave plantations, the point could be made as told in the accounts of the slaves, that their biggest obstacles was not overcoming the slave master but overcoming the fear of advancing one's self. Slaves like Harriet Jacobs did not seem to take their condition personally. She did not write her narrative to get revenge or to expose her handlers: but to end the slave trade. How could someone under extreme punishment and constant fear not harbor hatred in their hearts unless she or he had come to the realization that the real battle is within their heart? The slave narratives and protest literature of the period, revealed that black people, slave or free had a proper understanding of what it took to be free. They knew that freedom was not a questions of geography because the laws kept extending the boundaries of freedom all the way to Canada and even when a slave escaped or was set free, they risked being re-enslaved in a so called free state. Just as the slave narratives began with the revelation of the writer's inner struggles, it was clear that the slaves knew the need for the development of an intellect of resistance which posed many epistemological questions, the answers to which did not easily reveal themselves. As the slaves organized revolts, rebellions and escapes, they set themselves around fundamental questions and not mundane ones. Does today's community organizer read, and is he or she aware of the personal journey required for someone seeking to organize to fight oppression today?

However, even now, there remains so many books that have not been read or discussions that have not been had regarding the critical thinking and reasoning skills necessary for liberation, advancement and building models of self-determination. Black people have a strong legacy of resistance against oppressive government that predates 1776, but it is more recent events that give rise to uprisings in the streets of America. This is partly because of an amnesia on the part of African Americans who have lost or never obtained a revolutionary sense of history—which is cultural and intellectual as well as social and political. The rise of black resistance and the urban revolts that have occurred recently were blamed by others on a so-called rising tide of socialism rather on a historic opposition to state oppression. Socialism had nothing to do with the deaths of George Floyd or Tamir Rice, but when the spin doctors get finished with the narrative Karl Marx was behind the entire event—as if black people need Marx to organize, or need his words to justify their actions. While Tim Keller and other white Christians need some western construct to justify their actions on behalf of others, black people do not need such justifications when facing naked white racism. African Americans want what other people want: to pursue happiness unhindered by government. Yet many scholars believe that it is government that is the problem! It's the black famers and the black businessmen suffer at the hands of discriminatory practices with the government's endorsement, so the marching in the streets has more to do with the use of government to accomplish discriminatory social outcomes. It is a fact that Huey Newton studied Nietzsche and employed many of his ideas, but he didn't need Nietzsche any more than a Martin Luther King needed a Gandhi. Intellectually speaking, as told by the writings of David Walker, William Wells Brown and Henry Highland Garnet, black people always illustrated the contradiction between slavery and freedom, Christianity and capitalism. In fact, black folks, themselves, are walking contradictions and as soon as they show up organized to a school board meeting or county commission meeting, there is going to be a major disruption in the plans of the governing board. Any mass voter registration spells defeat for the ruling elite of any party—be it right or left.

The mass mobilization of Africans Americans in the wake of the police violence and unreconcilable differences between the people and the local government made some whites feel left out. They had nothing to protest about and no cause to fulfill. They were not satisfied with a good economy and booming housing market. They felt a need to mobilize: but against whom? I think a lot of jealousy on the part of conservative groups was that their organization was ineffective when it appeared that black organizing was paying off in the form of newly elected candidates, public policy reforms and other cosmetic changes like the removal of statues and Confederate flags. What happens when Nietzsche agrees with the Black Panthers? Robert E. Lee is removed from the town square, but this does little to challenge the contradictions in American society. Frederick Douglass intimated a deep feeling of extreme contempt for American hypocrisy in his speech *What to the Slave is the 4th of July* and in his *Appeal, David Walker* distinguishes America as being the most brutal among so called *civilized nations*. However, what makes America's social construct an absurdity are its assertions of freedom that are made against the historic backdrop of slavery and then Jim Crow. Slavery robbed black people of the ability organize around revolutionary ideas. Slave revolts were mostly a major threat to the institution of slavery not because of its imminent threat to national security but to the instability it could bring to a southern way of life that was built on slavery—a fact that was reintroduced in the Montgomery Bus boycott when the homes of southern whites were threatened with disillusion when the Negro women could not superintend them anymore. The dependency of the southern home on the negro was so great as told by W.E.B. Du Bois in his essay on the Negro mother, that during the bus boycott many of the Negro maids were given cars at the expense of their white employers. Because the issues of slavery and Jim Crow have gone unreconciled, black people still feel a need to keep this fact before the American consciousness: that America tends to mischaracterize or dismiss the causes of the people that it has oppressed and uses the conflict to the benefit of a small few. Some say: "let's not mention slavery, intersectionality, critical race theory, systemic racist or social justice because these are Marxist!" These same people avoid mentioning the need to read the classics such as Uncle Tom's Cabin that reveal the horrors of the slave trade in a much more vivid light than a CRT exercise. The concepts of liberty, fraternity and equality are not new to the African nor African Americans, but the murder of black men by cops and the complaints of black people that follow are reclassified as gripes or insults and not legitimate constitutional assertions. Yet African Americans have suffered the most when trying to obtain those things freely offered to others because they may have falsely assumed that blacks would be given what could only be obtained through *struggle*—not in a Marxist sense but an African one! One of the worst things for black people is when they are taught that it was white men making decisions that secured rights that otherwise would not have been given. History teaches us that slavery posed major philosophical problems for the founding fathers and segregation was the thorn in the side of many American presidents. My question to them is: why was the struggle to end slavery and Jim Crow so troubling if it did not involve the compromise of a vital economic and social advantage?

From whence does the slave embrace the call for freedom? The promises of the U.S. Constitution are ancient when it comes to African culture but enter the ethos of slave resistance from the American Revolution, the Underground Railroad, the La Amstad Mutiny, the Haitian Revolution and then the revolts of Denmark Vessey, Gabrielle Prosser, Madison Washington and Nat Turner—which were some of the first instances of community action on the part of slaves. The slaves did not listen to white men and try to imitate them. Instead, the Africans and indigenous people of color were already free and wished to return to their previous state and advance without compromising their integrity. Not to mention the businesses, networks and organizations that were started by ex-slaves and freedmen in the North and abroad which testify to the adaptability of colored people emerging from slavery. Emerging from slavery was not as challenging as maintaining a sense of self and a degree of historical integrity about advancement. The great organizers of the colored man during slavery was Prince Hall, Absoloam Jones, Richard Allen and Frederick Douglass. One of the first to attempt the organization of free blacks in a political manner was Martin Delany who basically stated that the same science that was necessary for the uplift of white people is needed to uplift black people. It is also noteworthy that Delany's descriptions of the dire conditions of free blacks in the north were strikingly similar to the conditions in our inner cities and among many black people today. Delany emphatically stated that it is the science of political organization that we seek to teach; the ability and courage to come together for the purpose of accomplishing self-interest through established and conventional means—which promotes a group's political action. Delany described the conditions of free blacks in the north to be no different than slaves in the south. Richard Allen, Prince Hall and Absalom Jones were organizers of local resistance efforts aimed at organizing black people – both free and slave – to abolish the slave trade and it is in the spirit of these and many others that we write this book. Those mentioned above and many others established businesses of various sorts as an outgrowth of their quest to liberate their people and their organizations had a cooperative effort. It is not until we look at our struggle not as a class struggle but as a matter of life or death that we appreciate the nature of our condition and the gravity associated with political organization.

Lazarus and the Rich Man

Today's societal conflicts are looked at by some as being a battle between the classes: the rich and the poor. Yet hidden within this so called class struggle is the battle to be recognized. Even within the black community there is a division between the boule, the "highbrows" and the ghetto or the hood. The light skinned versus dark skinned is a major conflict between all colonized people. Wherever colonialism has persisted, so has the issue of complexion both in the islands, the Americas and abroad. The battle in the west is similar to the biblical stories. Geographically speaking, the experiences of the co-called inner city and those of the suburbs somewhat resembles the divisions and antagonisms of ancient Judea in the days of Jesus.

Interestingly enough, Jesus does not even mention the overreaching presence of the Roman occupation and colonial domination. We can also incorporate the story of the Good Samaritan. Yet the questions posed in the stories of Jesus is one of citizenship, brotherly love, community and not merely nationality. Who is my neighbor: a question which spoke to the divisions of the day. While in the scriptures these two groups, the rich and poor, are seen as adversaries or antagonistic toward each other, peaceful coexistence is possible. In the story of the parable of Lazarus and the Rich Man, the poor can exist without having to steal or take from the rich and the rich can live well without stealing what little bread the poor can muster. In His illustrations, Jesus gives us an example that is meaningful to our efforts. As Jesus tells the story, there existed two men as neighbors: Lazarus who was poor and the rich man in whose driveway the poor man dwelled. The rich man lived a lavish lifestyle and Lazarus was a homeless man with no visible means of income. They coexisted as neighbors and do not seem to have been antagonistic toward each other. The rich man did not mock Lazarus or call him the reason for all social problems nor did Lazarus bring accusations against the rich man for not sharing his wealth. We do not know how Lazarus became poor nor do we know how the rich man became rich. However, their coexistence, no matter how close in proximity, was inconsequential to the position of the other. They lived a peaceful co-existence. Lazarus did not steal from the rich man nor did he try to run a game or use force or sympathy on the rich man to take what was not his. All Lazarus wanted was the leftovers, but his desires went unanswered. The rich man died and was buried, but Lazarus was taken into Abraham's bosom where he suffered no more. The rich man went to hell and there he was able to see Lazarus and ask for help. Now, the tide has turned and the proximity seems similar to the condition on earth yet the gulf between remained impassable. However this time, Lazarus was not permitted to address him. Abraham speaking for Lazarus stated that Lazarus' helping him was impossible because there was a great gulf fixed that made welfare and financial aid, philanthropy, charity and even reparations impossible in hell. The rich man did not see Lazarus on earth perhaps because, to him, Lazarus was invisible. However, in death, the earthly situation or circumstance is reversed and it is upon this principle that we speak! We are not trying to save Lazarus: we're trying to save a few rich people from making the terrible and eternal mistake of being so shortsighted that they miss an opportunity to contribute to the well-being of others without having to lose anything. The Or Else Factor does not involve robbery or thievery. "Or Else" is about the confronting those who deliberately use government force to maintain power. Because the government contains the people's money, using government to do good is not an act of private interest, it's for the people! A person can do what they choose with his or her own money, but the resources generated by the government's revenue are for the people of the community!

Introduction

"It is said to be a hard and difficult task to organize and keep together large numbers of the Negro Race for the common good. Many have tried to congregate us but have failed, the reason being that our characteristics are such as to keep us apart than together." *Marcus Garvey, An Appeal to the Conscience of the Black Race to See Itself, Written from Tombs Prison, New York City, August 14, 1923*

Violence in the nation's urban areas are not surprises to those who know better. Cities have anticipated various forms of social unrest since the 50s and 60s that would be caused by many different possible social events. From the aftermath of the murder of George Floyd to the failed but impactful insurrection on the nation's capital, social unrest has always been a part of the American pathos. This was anticipated by the founding fathers. In the Federalist Papers No. 21, Alexander Hamilton stated when speaking of the possibility of a D.C. takeover or any usurpation: *A successful faction may erect a tyranny on the ruins of order and law, while no succor could constitutionally be afforded by the Union to the friends and supporters of the government.* This meant that even at the birthing of our nation, the founding fathers recognized no federal mechanism that could be employed to stop a state militia from totally trampling on the rights of its citizens. Later, during the Jim Crow era, the Colfax Massacre and the burning of Black Walk Street would serve as major examples of whites using violence to stop black progress as the federal government did nothing. So what good is non-violent organizing when whites use guns to get their way if conventional means fail? But no one can deny that things are getting more heated as corporate profits ascend to unprecedented heights. In fact, the use of military grade weapons and hardware by municipalities as well as the use of paramilitary techniques by rioters is a well-documented fact. The civil rights workers like James Farmer (Rising Tide of Black Resistance) in America noticed that, like in South Africa, the local police were becoming more militarized to prevent urban rebellions. This is because the white power structure historically intensified its efforts as black protests intensified. Whites have never backed down from blacks nor shown any sense of letting up without the potential to lose money and their way of life in the process. This is critical when understanding how coronavirus can proliferate as well as how successful community organizing can be posed. "Hit them in the wallet rather than scare them with possible violence. Take away their conveniences, luxuries, pleasures and leisure." There is no evidence that the white power structure was relenting or surrendering in any fashion to the advances of black protest even in the 60s—despite the march from Selma to Montgomery and the March on Washington. It was the government, the same government responsible for racism, that intervened with legislation, resolutions and policy changes. It is for this reason, that non-violence becomes the most reasonable and logical approach, because white violence is relentless and absolute in accomplishing its goal. It is for this reason, that oppression drives even a wise man mad because it makes no reasonable or logical sense except to maintain one groups control over another group. A strong show of force does nothing to stop "the man" from doing as he chooses and he does not mind reminding you of this fact! There must be some threat posed to his money or his well-being.

Today's protesters have not learned this lesson. Standing with fists in the air shouting the chants of the civil rights past do nothing to move the power structure, but an exploitation of the state's weaknesses makes non-violent political negotiation the main means of resistance and advancement. Until the 2020 presidential election and the expenditure of hundreds of millions of dollars in states like Georgia, the vote remained the least utilized means of change in our republic. Georgia was successful because of the millions of dollars directed there—something that had never been done before. However, many moderate Republicans afraid of the recklessness of former President Trump could flood back into the Democratic Party and take it back to its racist roots—a phenomenon similar to the fallout of the Election of 1878 between Rutherford B. Hayes and Samuel Tilden. In a highly contested race, which involved questionable election results in three states and a close electoral count, Hayes pledged to end federal control of the south and promised to restore power to the local governments. The Democrats became Republicans and the Negroes who had nowhere to go were simply pushed out of office. This meant that justice would no longer be in the hands of the federal government and went back into the hands of the former slave masters who, with impunity, enforced the brutal campaign against Negro progress called Jim Crow. This may very well happen again considering that, historically, the issue of race outweighs any loyalties assumed along other lines. It is for this reason that there must be intense organization at the local level. We cannot fall for the propaganda, even by some of our own, who claim that black folk cannot organize. The problem is that "organization" has been so mystified by white supremacy and those who believe in it, that we lack a scientific step by step method of doing it. Love and struggle go hand in hand!

It's time for members of the public to take matters into their own hands. Not to burn buildings or stop freeways, but to become citizen scientists: committed to learning government and mastering its concepts. Epistemologically speaking, the closer a people are to information about themselves and their environment, the more effective their efforts to organize. The world is not prepared for an informed black community and neither are we! However, we must be prepared for sweeping change that will come when more people become better informed by their own exposure, research and analyses. A person being *informed*, as opposed to simply being educated, often determines the extent to which a person gets involved in anything. Typically, the more informed a person is about a topic or situation, the more likely they are to be engaged in an effective way. An informed person is not afraid of politicians, television cameras or confrontations with others. So, the goal of those in power is to limit how much the public knows about an issue and also to limit the opportunities to become informed. An informed community is an organized community because it is *knowledge* that unifies them and not fantasies, personalities, dogmas and ideology that is hard to understand. However, there are so many forces at work to misinform or channel the attention of the community into unhealthy directions. Right now so much of our perception of things comes from consensus shaping institutions that try to influence the masses not to act or confuse them into acting contrary to their best interest. Since Trump lost the election and even before, there seemed to be serious disturbances in the heights of government and political elites because he created serious problems. For some reason, neither parties were paying attention to grassroots community organizing and instead seemed to be focused on commercials and online media options until the death of George Floyd. The distancing of political candidates from the public, even in local elections, makes for a further bridging and distancing of the elected official from those who hold them accountable. City council meetings and county commission meetings would become battle zones and local governments began limiting opportunities to address their bodies which resulted in the enactment of uncontested policies because members of the public were excluded from the meetings.

Social Distancing, Dismissal and Denial

For some time the academic world has been under attack. A failure of outreach on the part of our nation's public institutions is vital to the distancing that is taking place in society. For example, in the past, in Montgomery, Alabama, its major employer Maxwell Air Force base used to flood the community with airmen and airwomen and the entire city embraced the influx of military personnel that came to the city. However, today, there is little or no effort to rekindle the relation. Also, the nation's colleges and universities are struggling to build public outreach programs for the purpose of doing field research. Universities now have millions of dollars in research funding but with no means of reaching a community that it needs for deepened credibility. These universities find themselves confronting a society that does not trust its vaccines and programs because there is no relationship between them and the public. The same thing can be said about the police department and other auxiliaries. Even many churches are losing members and struggling for existence because they cannot encourage people to come to church while at the same time refusing to come to the people. This dismissal and denial has become the only social distancing our institutions want to implement. But it can eventually work in favor of community organization in ways that we'll discuss later.

COVID and the Temporary Loss of Consensus

President Trump was headed for a sure win but a virus spoiled the entire thing. A virus could not be insulted, intimidated or bought off. It had no feelings to hurt or dirty laundry to expose. This was truly a perfect storm which took down the most dynamic presidential machine in history. His camp had unity of action and thought. They were all for the same things and seemed not to mind existing outside of the moral perimeters. The President emboldened his followers to be bodacious and insulting. They exploited the distance that had been created by the previous administration who neglected to address the psychological needs of a significant population of living breathing people who felt they had no voice. The distancing is really felt at the national level with the national political parties but the consciousness of the people is rising without their presence to such a degree that these field directors must come with checks now even to get people to return their phone calls. The Wikileaks scandal and the exposure of the questionable practices of Cambridge Analytica and Facebook have revealed the emphasis placed on virtual intelligence methods by major corporate interests to influence the thinking of large populations of people rather than canvassing the people to see what they want. Yet there is a disturbance in the force! The hundreds of millions of dollars paid for algorithms that predict human behavior at the local level have all been thrown out of kilter and are pretty much useless because COVID-19 has all but ended our social predictability. Because we are not spending money in our usual fashion but are doing it online or curbside, it is hard to predict our habits, which means the web or the net has to adjust with new algorithms to get us to buy stuff. Also, the marketing strategies used by mostly Republican candidates were made worthless because they were set to rely on low voter turnout and single day voting, not voting access that's spread out over long periods of time. The defeat of the Voting Rights Act and the various forms of voter ID laws actually worked to the advantage of local organizers because it better unified the voting process and made it easier. Clean voter rolls made for cleaner elections and the impact that voter suppression efforts would have on local voter turnout, especially in urban areas is something the Republicans did not anticipate. Also unexpected acceptance of Black Lives Matter into the corporate ethos of many companies has also temporarily made for conversations that otherwise would be closed to discussion. The door is open for grassroots movements because many people do not wish to labeled as a racist and wish to avoid undo attention paid to their actions.

White Supremacy; A National Stupidity

The essence of grassroots community organizing is about life, liberty and the pursuit of happiness. Before *group organizing* can occur, the organizers, as well as the inner core of organization leadership, must understand individualism and self-knowledge before understanding group action. A republic comprises of individuals; all with their own rights to pursue goals as they see fit. However the problem is white supremacy which is barbaric, anti-logical and anti-republic. Racism and prejudice thwarts the entire system and makes America a savage and primitive state because white supremacy is not based on a standard of reasonableness but on mere DNA. Self-knowledge assists one in accomplishing the aims of the republic, but group action is a form of self-defense to something that should be unnecessary under normal circumstances. White supremacy is so anti-American and anti-patriotic that the nation cannot stand on normal grounds but on pretensions and mythology. So what is it about self-knowledge that is so important? Self-knowledge is critical because all successful organization efforts are led by informed and knowledgeable leaders who are rooted in their identity and they simply encourage the community to become informed about themselves and their issues. A person with self-knowledge does not hesitate or second guess his intuitions but is assertive in positive action. Self-knowledge will give a leader the moral rooting needed to understand that all progress is group orientated and not individually realized. At the present state, true community organization is very difficult because the so-called leaders have not been trained nor taught the ropes of self-knowledge or self-interest or political organizing. While they may be notoriously self-centered or down right criminal in their office, simple aspects of personal political personality, character and habits escapes them. Many of today's black politicians are incredibly simple, distant and undeserving of their office because they won a popularity contest which qualified as an election. They were members of a fraternity or sorority or come from some family legacy which has never translated into anything meaningful for the masses of people. They claimed to be "for the people" but compromise their own communities' interest as soon as money is involved. How many politicians have gone to jail for ethics violations in the past decade and who has been the biggest casualty to their defeat? Their districts are the poorest and the most crime ridden because they know little of governance or urban planning because there are no schools that teach the skills necessary for good leadership and enterprise building. However, Steve Bannon has a degree in Urban Planning and understands well the conditions that dictate it.

The science of political and community organizing are more distant from us now than they were during slavery. Yet other groups can operate at a level of organization that blacks can only dream without the vote because the cultural element of organization has been maintained by them while it has not been reinforced with black people. People from other countries come to America without the right to vote or even a grasp of the language and set up businesses and make ways for themselves. This is because it is culture that teaches these things and not a school. It is not a fact that black folks cannot trust each other, it is the fact that we do not know how to organize ourselves to be represented and the black power elite make sure that we never organize because the first order of business would be to get rid of them if we did organize! Blacks are the least productive minority group and the government helped by enacting the Hart-Celler Act of 1965 which allowed for thousands of preferred immigrants to enter the country with incentives while Patrick D. Moynihan concluded that the black family was breaking up because of slavery! The politicians, pastors and leaders are no more informed than the people who elected them and it shows by their inability to solve systemic problems of crime, poverty and education. The more informed and politically educated the community, the less appeal ineffective leaders will have to the people who elected or selected them. So within the black community there is an internal force which simply seeks to keep the people miseducated, ignorant and off balance, which makes community organization virtually impossible. The ineffective leadership knows that when the people become informed, their power is over and they will be replaced with a representative of the common consciousness of the community. An informed group does not feel intimidated by local government neither do they feel inferior to others. A person does not feel inferior to one who is his or her intellectual equal!

It's About Life, Liberty and Property

Saul Alinsky stated that every community is already organized prior to the organization coming into the community, but those who organized it did so for the benefit of the existing power structure and not the people. Most *preferred* or *suburban* or gentrified neighborhoods are planned and strategically located to obtain a certain political and economic end, but are, at the same time, powerless against a social movement or community action initiative which challenges city hall. In the past, discriminatory zoning laws and restrictive covenants prevented certain types of movements within a city, but now the opportunity is wide open for the suburbs to become ground zero for community protests, rallies and boycotts even if the intended target is downtown. Just like the suburbs, even the ghetto is planned and serves as a type of swamp in a city's economic and political ecosystem. But when people become informed, they take an interest in the laws, rules and policies that they are under. Now it matters what the law is and how it is interpreted. So when it is time to organize a community, it is actually an attempt to reorganize it out of the previously established condition. A community, organized against itself and its interests, is simply a herd of arthropods with conflicting passions, ideas and motivations who have been trained to enter and exit organizations based on their sentiments and emotions. They are angry, mad, driven to tears but are no more capable of effectuating change because they are not informed of the true nature of their condition – the characterization of which must be converted into legal terms! For example, a city's attempt to exercise eminent domain over a community or a parcel of private property might be a constitutional *taking* of property; but it is a *taking* just the same! "Taking" is a legal term which could equally apply to the city's issuance of a liquor license to an establishment in your neighborhood that will average 15 police calls a month, not to mention a barrage of stray bullets. The building of a paper mill or fertilizer plant which might contaminate the local water supply is truly a taking so maybe the mayor or county commission might want to sample some of the local catfish grown in the polluted river. So the community organization becomes a defender of the rights of its members under the constitution and the law.

Yet what is being taught through the organizer are the civil tenants of our nation and not some other nation or idea foreign or hostile to it. Community organizing is about teaching the civic duty of being an *American* in the most authentic form and I am convinced that many so called patriot groups, while grassroots, have no idea what it means to be *American*. These groups have organized around ideals, ideology, religion or hate but not information and truth. These groups use violence and intimidation and fear because they make no sense in civil discourse. I can tell by their support of the government when black people protest and their protest of government when things tend to go in the favor of black people seeking justice. For instance, when dirty cops are exonerated by the justice system there is little interest by patriot groups (although they claim to be anti-government), but when dirty cops are fired and prosecuted, those seeking justice are called "anti-police" and these subversive groups become gun-toting mobs. However, the trigger for these group's activities is the perceived constitutionality of the moving party's claim! To be specific and undogmatic, Thomas Jefferson cited life, liberty and the pursuit of happiness as being the aims of our republic and the same goes for the community organization who seeks enforcement of the law as it was written. Those against the community are lawless and are responding to our inaction of constitutional grounds. While my left-wing friends might cringe at this, when in juxtaposition with the 14th Amendment, *happiness* is defined constitutionally in terms of *property*. Effective community organizing is not about ideology or ideals which are not measurable. Instead, it is about simply converting group demands into property interest terms such as in material, personal, real, intellectual or business. A study of what property is in a legal sense helps out a lot when trying to get the people to understand what is at stake or what could be gained from community action. Not to be partisan, but it is at this point that we depart from typical utopic radical ideological organizing, sponsored ever-so-gloriously by certain high profiles groups, and embrace the smooth waters of practical politics where the people get what they want without having to understand a lot of European political or social theory. The Black Panther Party for Self Defense is one of the greatest examples of the possibilities and pitfalls of community organizing. However they were known more for the pictures of its members holding shotguns, sporting afro hairstyles and wearing leather jackets rather than its organization of the community in regards to nutrition, education, healthcare and security. The origin of the BPP was in Lowndes County, Alabama but the Lowndes County Freedom Organization (LCFO) was about voting rights and community building and not fighting the police. The BPP was as pro 2nd Amendment as any patriot group but the fact they were black eclipsed the rights they were seeking to protect! As their agenda expanded, so did the nature of their persecution by the government. Soon, the Panthers were dissolved and nothing or nobody could bring them back. It is my opinion that when they began to embrace socialism that an inseparable wedge was placed between them and the people they sought to protect. Helping the Vietnamese and other oppressed people is cool but you cannot spread yourself thin nor get involved on other people's matters that we lose the home front. As Voltaire stated: Cultivate your own garden. The world might change but right now we are concerned with city hall and not solving global oppression!

Ideas But No Ideology!

It is an interesting thought experiment to analyze the impact that social movements have on the opposing community's perception of reality, especially when it comes to the interpretation and definition of words. Recently, several Southern Baptist pastors and seminary presidents signed a resolution not to teach certain topics in their seminaries – as if the people would not be tempted to learn the forbidden concepts just because they were prohibited to do so by some jive seminary presidents! What kind of education would it be if the president of the school dictated what was being taught? Out of nowhere the Southern Baptist Convention sought to condemn slavery along with critical race theory! How pointless and telling this gesture was, that no consideration or credibility was to be given to any ideas foreign to their own. To organize black people, one need not be intimidated if he or she does not know the meaning of words like *hegemony*, intersectionality or critical race theory as if the restriction of teaching these subjects would somehow diminish the interest in the social implications of the terms. Nor do blacks need Marx or Engels to gain inspiration to overthrow oppression. As opposed to getting wrapped up in social theory or even social justice rhetoric, the community organizers need to know what they want to accomplish and how to get it within the legal concept of property rights instead of social theory. As opposed to being lumped into the ever expanding world of the left wing, the community organization should speak in clear legal terms and not the mystical and glorified rhetoric of the so-called revolutionary past. There is no need for visual displays of defiance nor are the fashionable aesthetics of agitation needed such as wearing a Che Guvera T-Shirt or a black power symbol. There is no need for Democrats in Dashikis either! There is no need for fists in the air, chants or banner cries. The community organizer should say: "No we are not socialist, and no we are not BLM…We are citizens, legally entitled to these things and this is what we want… now!" There is little saber rattling or protesting but pure unadulterated pressure placed on those in power to follow the demands of the people is the objective. "We want this lady fired and we want an end to nepotism…we want the city manager fired…now!" Community organizing does not require reimagining; it requires a conceptualization of the value of their desired goals. No one can paint a picture for the organizer because it is the people who decide the goals. "We don't want the government doing this or that and we want to exist without having the city sticking its noise in what we are doing…we want dirty cops fired and the chief of police fired…now." Malcom X, Martin Luther King, the Black Panthers and other groups had good runs but could not build organizations that could effectively outlive them. After the movement subsided, black people began to lose heart as these organizations expanded their emphasis and today's organizers should keep it as local and simple as possible. I always say, keep it local! Even now, black people know little of Marxism, Nkrumaism, socialism or dialectics and in my opinion, they don't have to know these things to get stuff done at the local level. To organize, you do not need a flamboyant or charismatic speaker, violence or mass marches…you need someone who can articulate the issues and give headway on how each individual can act in the best interest of the community. To create a national identity, there might be a need for a heroic figure, but in community organizing the less appealing and the less dogmatic the leader the better. There is no need for a martyr or sacrificial lamb to make a point or bring attention to a cause. It is our hope that practical measures would make the need for a dead black body unnecessary.

My thesis is that the civil rights efforts tanked when local organizations were lured into the national and global effort to free all oppressed people at the expense of the local issues which remained unsolved. Osageyfo Kwame Nkrumah stated that black people in America will not be free until Africans are free, but to abandon the local effort in favor of the global one neglected the first struggle, which was at home. Malcom X said that "we cannot expect black people to change until white people change." Building a healthy exchange of efforts whereby the local effort is accomplished is critical to understanding power; which is always centralized. Our research has shown, black people vote in their best interest in national elections and state elections, but fail and are least effective when addressing local issues that impact everyday life. This makes city hall, not the United Nations the ground zero of all community and political organizing.

Free Enterprise, Free Expression and Free Thought

We will steer the discussion in the direction of free thought. Thomas Jefferson wished to be remembered for three things; the writing of the freedom of Religion clause of the Virginia Constitution, the authorship of the Declaration of Independence and the establishment of the University of Virginia. Intimated into the Virginia Constitution is the assumption that man's mind is the primary tool of advancement, and that ideas must be free from the restraints which tend to come from an out-of-control religious oligarchy. The control of the oligarchy is centered on enslaving the mind—thinking! An organized people are thinkers and their thoughts are their personal intellectual property. Before freedom of speech, there is freedom of thought and the plans of the community organizer must be well thought out! Constitutionally speaking, there are many different types of property, the protection of which people can organize around: including real, personal, intellectual and business interests which cannot be taken by the government without due process of law. Yet thoughts remain the property of the individual. The protection and promotion of varying forms of property pose different challenges when threatened by outside forces like corrupt cops, evasive city planning projects and invasive government intrusions. For example, questions of redlining, fair housing, affordable housing and zoning are issues of real property but the treatment of city workers is a professional business interest question. Police brutality is about government sanctioned public corruption and criminal enterprise that infringes on personal property rights protected by the U.S. and state constitutions. The famous U.S. Supreme Court Cases of Mapp v. Ohio and Terry v. Ohio had to do with questions of government intrusion into the lives of black people. These issues involved questions of what constituted illegal searches and seizures. Yet today, national organizations like Black Lives Matter allow for the narrative to shift away from the law and to a nebulous issue called *social justice* instead of using more generalized terms such as government corruption, criminal enterprise and matters of constitutional law. While a white person might not be criminally profiled, the violation of one's rights can happen to anyone, and the black community's call for justice is no different than that of others who might not seek to organize as a group to address a problem. When a community organizes itself, it is to protect some interest found in the U.S. or state constitution, city ordinance or government regulation or oversite. The only question is one of means and not ends. Organizing requires the objectification of desired goals and an organization's list of demands must be reduced to basic and simple terms that the average person can understand. The "hell no we won't go" movement was as much a rally against local draft boards who were intentionally drafting black men from the movement to die to Vietnam as it was a protest against American foreign policy in China. Also the national Voting Rights Act was created to stop the many lawsuits being filed at the local and state levels which were backing up the courts to the point that other cases not be heard. Community organizing is not simply marching or "raising hell" or throwing bricks or gas bombs through windows. People who do so are troublemakers with undefined goals. It's unchecked aggression that never translates into a protection of property but rather, the destruction of other people's property. They come from outside the affected community after some local crises develops, taking things outside the scope of the local dynamic – and some people are very good at it. Instead, community organizing is about bringing facts to the table to solve a problem or promote an agenda that is real and immediate. Saying that struggle is eternal scares people and makes them think they are joining some cult or radical group and fear becomes the motivator instead of truth. But a lot of people really lack knowledge of how to get things done and educating them on how to get what they want is a major part of organizing to obtain power.

A biblical definition of *power* in the Greek New Testament is to have rights to become whatever one is inclined to have them be. These rights are not given by man, so it is out of the mayor's hands! Instead, power is given by God, which means that man has nothing to do with the bestowal of rights, but rights are vested in a person's being as an individual first and then extends to family and nation. Now in the bible, there were kings who were supreme, but America has no title of nobility. In a republic, power begins with the people and moves upward. In a republic, the people chose their executive who should remain a servant but we know this does not happen. Being an *individual* and being a *person* do not have the same meanings. The term *individual* does not mean anything in particular except but to be a part of or distinguished from a group, but being a *person* is specific and it is to a person that rights attach. A person can be a firm, organization and even a corporation and it should be remarked that the corporation becomes the political hydra that it is now once it was declared a person under the Fourteenth Amendment for the purposes of political activity (See Citizens United v. Federal Election Commission 558 U.S. 310). The main rationale of a corporation being "persona" is that it can own property and perpetuate the ownership of property to others after it is disillusioned. However, why is a collective of individual human beings not looked upon as being as powerful? Why are community organizations not treated with the same glamour as a Microsoft or Google?

Not a Question of Slavery, Poverty or Crime but Purpose

I often wondered why is seems taboo to mention the ills in the black community in any other context than as being an effect of slavery. Why can't we just admit failure in raising our kids except that such admissions play into the political hands of our enemies? I was very concerned that many social scientists and their

INTRODUCTION

consorts tend to blame crime in the black community on poverty, which is blamed on capitalism. Yet many of these same people do not seek to solve either the poverty or crime issue. What will solve the crime issue will simultaneously solve all the other ills in the black community. Information makes a person strong and kids who read above their reading levels do not execute other kids in the streets! We are prompted to mobilize when a white cop kills a black man because of the historic implications. Yet why is there not an organization around internal social issues like education, recreation and the theater? Why can we not march against ourselves? It seems that some people almost all of whom live outside the hood are comfortable with waiting on the coming of a new system while black people in the hood suffer a staggering death toll. Some even look at the deaths of our kids as being necessary in part due to a dystopic trajectory that this capitalist society is on and to that I say nonsense. A community where people are violent toward each other or where violence is an accepted pathological pattern is one that is organized against itself. The source responsible for the association between poverty and slavery is Patrick D. Moynihan's **The Negro Family:** *The Case for National Action*.[1] Moynihan's contention—which has become the Rosetta Stone for doing the social sciences in the ghetto—places the ultimate responsibility on the government to correct negative social pathologies in the hood. Until then, it is assumed that there is no action that can be taken and the body count mounts—even in cities with black elected officials and black staff in almost every branch of government. We do not have time to test evolutionary cultural theories nor do community organizers have to wait for state intervention in the form of programs to take control of a neighborhood. We don't have to sacrifice our young people for the sake of the group and the rights of the children do not give way to group need when the objective is to accomplish a particular goal. It never comes to this when organizing locally because the pressure put on government comes from the group interest. That is why knowledge of self is fundamental to existing in our republic and before one can love their neighbor they must first love self and seek to preserve self.

---

1. 1965 report written by Danial Patrick Moynihan, Assistant Secretary of Labor under the President Lyndon B. Johnson

CHAPTER 1
What Do We Want?

The basic needs of the citizen endures throughout the ages. According to the Delphic Manumission of ancient Greece, which was applicable in Jesus' day there was four things that made someone a slave:

1) Lack of Legal Rights
2) Liability to Seizure
3) Inability to choose one's activities
4) Lack of choice in determining residency

Are these factors not critical to addressing the needs of the community today? This sounds similar to the list of demands of the Black Panther Party or the Montgomery Improvement Association. It seems that when the police attack black people, it is to enforce one or all of these ancient aspects of enslavement and precepts to freedom. Just as in ancient times, these issues remain the essence of organizing today. In a republic, the individual must join his self to others in common interest to protect against infringements by the government. As stated in books like *Color of Law* by Richard Rothstein, the government is the biggest discriminator of people, and organizing against corrupt governments is the objective. Yet the founding fathers in the Federalist Papers warned against factionalism and local tyranny, which could grow naturally and unchecked in free societies to undermine minority groups. What makes racism prosper in America is the amount of freedom we have; to do basically as we choose with little hindrance from government; and to say as we choose and organize under whatever pretense that is not threatening to the peace and order. To limit factionalism, freedom must be limited. Yet in our times, community organizing typically takes place because some great imminent consequence to the community emerges from outside the environment. Some faction has taken over and commandeered local governments and is using it for some nefarious deed.

The Right To Organize

Africans are a people of order. Yet colonialism brought disorder and then reorganization under a colonialist system which lasts to this day. The Africans aboard the slave ship organized and in Haiti and the United States. Laws were passed and foreign policy was enacted not to support or recognize the gains made by revolting Africans. During slavery a moral question emerged when it was time to resist. The question involved the responsibility one had to the group; whether to run away and secure freedom for one's self or to remain and struggle as a group? However, now free, the question is more convoluted. An individual *person* has the right to worship, associate, speak, publish or redress grievances. An individual has the right to bear arms, form a militia and be free from being imposed upon in his home by housing military troops. He cannot be hindered or imposed upon with excessive bail and is free from illegal searches and seizures etc. Yet the issue which makes for organizing is something not mentioned in the U.S. Constitution but is implied—that is the right to think for one's self and then the need to associate based on logic and reason! Yet one man's thoughts cannot be imposed upon another and thus the division becomes one of thinking and not other external factors like race or ethnicity. When multiple persons are subject to the same threats of divestment of thought or some other liberty, the need for those affected to organize arises. If the community perceives a certain benefit in obtaining a certain goal such as the building of a library or playground, the need to organize emerges. Yet it seems too hard to get things done at the local level, especially when city councils now make you call in days before to be placed on the agenda. Even if there is a standard procedure for getting something done like naming a bridge or renaming a park, organizing outside of the procedural guidelines is necessary and sometimes civil disobedience is needed as well. Nevertheless, I think community organizing needs to be spelled out in clear and concise terms: life, liberty and the pursuit of happiness. Never forget that! A major mistake of the so-called Black Renaissance movement and the civil rights movement was that it was co-opted by socialists who wanted individual black people to forgo personal gain in hopes of every black person being free at one time. Hubert Harrison, a former socialist himself referred to these people as crabs in the bucket. However, the socialist failed because they could not find effective apologists among the Negro elite although they courted them heavily. Harrison observed that the Negro community in Harlem was already building its own infrastructure without the help of the government but these black business owners were being intimidated by outsiders who saw their businesses as a threat to mass action. Community organizing seldom involves the question of violence because organizing is by nature proactive rather than reactive. The entire non-violent technique of the civil rights era was taken from the play book of union organizers sympathetic to the socialist cause[1]. Because the average Negro, like now, knew little of the black academics and intellectuals trying to reach the people, it was hard for them to identify with the concepts and language used by those seeking to organize them from without. As opposed to waving banners and invoking

---

1. The idea of Haywards, that the capitalist system must be overthrown by "forceable means if necessary" and other socialist departures from violence is expressed in Harold Cruises' Crisis of the Negro Intellectual . See The Intellectual, and Force and Violence New York Review Books 2005 p.349

the memories of dead revolutionaries, community organizers must keep the mission clear and in familiar terms that are not threatening or do not require a lot of ideological posturing. Community organizers do not require the people to give up or sacrifice anything. Instead, what they want is nothing more than what others want and that is to pursue happiness without some busybody or evil doer injecting ulterior motives. When it is time to fight, it's time to fight and reading Franz Fanon, although advisable, is not necessary to move city hall! There is a such thing as becoming too religious or ideological in attempts to bring to people things that they should have anyway. I have seen good ideas fall because the package they were presented in was too eccentric, radical, religious, ideological or political. When it comes down to successful community organizing, it is best to keep it as basic as possible. What we want is no different than what other people want: life, liberty and the pursuit of happiness. We want shopping centers and economic development! The fundamental quest for black people is the same for all people: to pursue justice, love mercy and walk humbly with their God! However, what makes accomplishing these goals problematic is that white supremacy is illogical, unreasonable, unscientific, anti-republican, anti-capitalist, primitive, tribalistic, barbaric and anti-objective. In short, it makes no sense. Those black leaders who refuse to work in the best interest of the community are equally problematic. Making sense is useless against barbarians bent on maintaining power. Sometimes the hegemony or power structure will pick a dunce to show that they do not need intelligence or logic to control others, just a firm commitment to the objective which does not rule out violence as a means of keeping order and peace. Fanon did say that we should not take lightly the colonial forces because if they were prepared to do the genocide done in Africa, Asia and America by enslaving and killing millions, they are not far removed from totally annihilating people of color. It is this understanding of the global situation that keeps the expectations of the local organizer realistic and objective. However black people have demonstrated that they are not afraid to bleed and die for the rights of the republic and as James Baldwin said, black people are not afraid of anything anymore!

Whites and status quo elitist blacks must be voted out of office and pressured into conformity to the will of the community organization. Against such nonsense as white supremacy there is no answer because white supremacy is anti-intellectual and can only be enforced through violence. If Amendments need to be enacted, so be it and if home rule needs to be enforced, let it happen! But stay within the language framework of the system, even if you hate the system. Community organizing is not metaphysical nor is there any heavenly stakes involved. There are no divine callings other than the need to be the committed minority seeking truth! There is no mystic goal nor should there be. Community organizing is about using what you have to get what you want. You do not have to wear African colors, fly black nationalist flags or sing Zion songs. However, what you do need is a plan and a strategy for getting what you want because you will get what you deserve regardless. A community organizer does not seek to change the habits of the people but use whatever habits they have to their advantage and against city hall.

Ok What Do You Want?

A lot of people who try to organize are not prepared to answer this question when it is posed, especially if it is posed before a fight or organizational mobilization occurs. Politicians want to know if you are real, if you are serious and if you can be of some benefit or detriment to them. There is a time to be specific and then there is a time to be general in your discussion of objectives. A community organizer, once elected by the people to organize them, must be prepared to give a response when asked: what is the reason for their action. Anybody can get mad but seldom does that anger transfer into positive action that gets results. "We want a speed limit sign at the corner…we want this principle at this school fired….we want our property taxes raised or we want this night club closed down." The organization must possess data supporting their position and have a list of concessions within themselves in case negotiations are in order. The give and take is necessary but some things are non-negotiable because it is a matter of life and death. The organization needs to identify those things that are deal breakers, the things that are deliverables and the things that are non-essential.

Sometimes it is not easy defining what the community wants to take place. Crime is too big a topic but the removal of a trap house on the corner of 5th and Elm is doable! Everything might hinge on a city council vote or county planning meeting so being present or having representation at meetings is critical. However, there is nothing more impactful than holding up a councilperson at his or her car in the parking lot of a grocery store or visiting the business of a county commission person and demanding a reason for his or her vote on granting a contract to a certain business. The people need a lobbyist but who has time to wait in boring meetings only for them to table your issue or adjourn sine die! Determining what the people want can be difficult if you look at black people as being some type of tropical fish needing special attention rather than being objective in addressing issues. The black community is not monolithic, yet they vote that way because the needs of the republic are across the board. Garvey said above, our universal response to the same conditions is because of their unique history and not some deficiency associated with the color of their skin.

All politics are local, yet we learn through the UNIA, SNCC and other groups of the civil rights movement that getting a bigger picture of the global problem helps with understanding the magnitude of the issue. The Black Panther Party and many of the student groups found education critical to understanding the big picture. The association between knowledge and freedom, and slavery and ignorance goes back to slavery but knowledge is as critical now as it was then. Yet high school and college students make the best organizers because their access to information that common people might not have time to research is readily available to them. Sometimes discussion in class or events occurring on campus give rise to political action. Sure the more informed one is the more strategic they will be in organizing.

The Origin of Black on Black Crime

It was not until the coming of the Arab and the European that African began to enslave African. Chenau Achebe stated in his book *Things Fall Apart*, that Africans started killing Africans when the European came and used religion, money and weapons to lure Africans to fight each other in a way unheard of before that time. Yet the main cause of battle was the forgoing of traditional ways for new ones; something that would have happened regardless of colonialism. Jomo Kenyatta, in Facing Mount Kenya, stated that it was the young people of his region who fell for the lures of the Europeans and saw fit to go against the tribal wisdom of the elders who told them to be very polite but very suspicious. Yet when the time arose, the Africans say it was necessary to fight other Africans in order to preserve their way of life. However, now communities find themselves having to organize against their own leaders, which, to some, is uncomfortable, but necessary. This is true especially in America with African Americans, but is not uncommon among the diaspora. It is for this reason that the study of American foreign policy toward Africa and American domestic policy toward African Americans is identical. Just like European interests aided in the demise of some African presidents and the support of others more deferential to western ideas, the same thing happens in America to the point that fights between black people can most of the time be traced back to some interest that lay outside the African American community. The same methods used to control Africans on their own continent are used to control blacks in America. The lot of a political prisoner in Africa is no different than an inmate's in Alabama pushing for sanitary and humane conditions in prison. Colonialism has lasted unto this day, so fighting city hall in Greensboro, Alabama is the same as fighting city hall in San Salvador or Oran, Algeria. The civil rights movement in America comprised of many local incidences that involved black people and the white power structure which was represented by the police. Yet it was the local police that instigated the Sharpeville Massacre in South Africa. Never mind the color of the police or the government official in question, when it is time to start organizing against oppression, the leaders must be mentally prepared to accept the fact they are confronting their own blood brothers, frat brothers and sorority sisters, their mason brothers and their Eastern Star sisters or church members. Steven Cokely identified these types as the *Black Boule*, those blacks who have been trained to serve others and not themselves. These are people that have something to lose if the community advances, so approach them with care and understanding because they might already be compromised and will sabotage your plans. A lot of times, when a black person tells you "no" it is because they never had the authority to tell you "yes" anyway. Do what I heard former state representative Alvin Holmes say one day: "We don't want to be told no by a black person, we want to talk to the white man in charge of the black folks telling us no."

Community Reorganization

A community is already organized prior to the organizer coming on the scene. So his or her job as an organizer is to undue years of conditioning that had come before him or her. The community organizer is coming against a system that has used force to subdue and organize the community in a way that supports the system. Force through intimidation, selective policing, firings, and sanctioning are all part of the game city hall plays. That is why those who are outsiders or those with the least to lose make the best community organizers. During the movement, the confrontations usually were instigated by some infraction committed by ordinary blacks against some facet of Jim Crow etiquette; which meant typically that some black person stepped outside of their lot in the local social order. Even to this day, some blacks instinctively go to the back of the room, or assume an inferior posture to whites. They laugh when there is nothing funny and they are oversensitive so as not to offend or to accommodate someone of another race. They do this to show that they can be trusted not to disrupt the social order. In churches, black ushers wear white gloves and collect the offering with one hand behind their backs; a practice that dates back to slavery when the slaves were called upon to collect church offerings. The white gloves were to show they had not touched the money and the hand behind the back is to prevent the other hand from ripping off the offering as well. Most lynching like that of Emmett Till occurred under these circumstances. Looking at a white man in the eye or whistling at a white woman was punishable by the most horrible death. So to fight Jim Crow, some of the most abominable things imaginable were done to defy the status quo. Saul Alinsky stated in his book *Rules for Radicals* that community organizing is about being irreverent. We say community organizing is about finding one's place in society and stepping outside of it. It is the very side stepping or overstepping of one's prescribed bounds which makes for the criminal act of organizing. Organizing is the biggest threat to public corruption and organized crime. While black people were constantly harassed by the police for whatever reason, clashes with police grew out of black people's resistance to mistreatment. Violence on the part of police makes armed and violent self-defense a moral imperative. A black person in LA or Detroit did not need to read Fanon to understand this fact. It was quite common for young people to be the first to stand their ground and they did not mind paying for it in the form of brutalization or arrests. The only reason why black people or any oppressed people would resist or fight back is that the oppressed seek to remove and replace the status quo with another, more beneficial, system. In Montgomery, the infamous Todd Road case wherein black people returning from a funeral were illegally invaded by warrantless and non-uniformed city police officers. The officers burst through the door and started roughing up people and received a butt whipping that was discussed even in the streets of Brooklyn when I visited there that same summer. Inside every human being is an intolerance of brutality and if pushed, the people will fight in some fashion. Community organizing is violent in that it uses persuasion *and* the "or-else" clause if logic and reason cannot do the job. King was very violent in his rhetoric when describing the economic tactics used to bring grocery stores, department stores and bread companies to its knees. Talking back to a white person, loitering, vagrancy, failing to step in the street when a white person was walking on the sidewalk or even looking a white person in the eye was worthy of police investigation. According to Ida B. Wells, even a black man owning a grocery store across the street from a white store was enough to earn them a visit from the local police, an arrest and a lynching. If a black man owned choice land, a stage coach or a fine horse he would be lynched for the very things that could have made him great. What makes racism so evil and diabolical is that it made the practical use of logic, reason and knowledge inconsequential to success or failure. Going to city council meeting armed with the right motive and the right cause does not ensure success. The community organization has to make threats and make good on them because they are continually left out of the decision making process. This is the oppression spoken of in the book of Ecclesiastes that makes even a wise man mad.

Community organizing is a bad word to some because it seeks to empower those who are supposed to be powerless, and anyone who organizes the poor is a big problem to the status quo. We don't want to overthrow the government but to take control of it and use it for our benefit. Defunding the police turns us into a dystopia or wasteland where the rich own the army and the police and the poor fight for and against each other. Yet removing dirty and flirty cops is an act of governance. Government is necessary because the administration of justice must be objective and not personal. Montgomery is suffering from local and personal conflicts that remain unresolved. Local vendettas and beefs are killing a lot of people but objective and strategic policing is the answer.

Making "Down Town" the Problem

Community organizers do not need to be directly impacted by the cause they are seeking to address. Too much emotion, personal animosity and involvement will cloud clear thinking and lead to logistical mistakes. Also, failing to associate a face with the problem is a major mistake. A community organizer does not seek to fight another group or political party, but should instead focus on one person. For example, victims of mass shootings build up a lot of emotion from the deaths and injuries of kids and teachers. The parents of these assassins remain hidden from view and the community even seeks to embrace the youthful killers in some type of empathetic manner. "Something went terribly wrong" in Sandy Hook or Columbine, whereas gang violence and local vendettas are the result of savage inner cities? Victims build mass movements around gun violence which eventually end with no new legislation or regulations passed. They shout, they call names and make threats but the NRA with their lobbyists keep the pressure on the legislators who hid behind the 2nd amendment while at the same time militarizing and disarming black people without discretion. Also, we never know who sold the guns to the killers. However, if the push was to fire local officials who should have been better prepared for emergencies, which is not an issue that depends on a community's reaction to a tragedy, then anybody can do this type of work without being directly impacted by gun violence. Whenever a gun goes off in the school, detectives, the DHR workers need to lose their jobs! Initially the political casualties of the gun safety issue are not tightening gun laws but the firing of local police and sheriff officers and administrators. A crisis like the school shootings can get multiple people fired which sends the message to those higher up. For policies to be changed, mayors have to lose their jobs and gun violence has to become the reason why city council persons lose elections. Have you ever seen a gun trafficker arrested and sent to prison? For any law to become just that law must be objective. The rules of community political engagement meet where the laws, policies and procedures become biased, illogical and against the good of individuals. Community organizing does not need to be in congruence with social or political theory nor is it utopic in nature. It does not take more time than necessary and there is no altruistic message in the people getting what they want. A safe school is no different than a safe shopping mall.

Good community organizing is very specific, tangible and temporary. To use a term from Saul Alinsky, there are no *phantasmagorias* or mysticisms. No travelers from the far east, no gurus or ascended masters in turbans claiming to have divine revelation from God. See where Jim Jones led the people—many of whom were black people heavily involved in the previous civil rights struggle. We are just a bunch of mad black people with a spot on plan to personify their problem in the form of the mayor whoever he or she might be. Black people have always fought police because the police have presented themselves as being the visual barriers to their advancement and there has never been a time when city hall was not hostile to the advancement of black people—even in towns where blacks are the majority. Arbitrary miscarriages of justice like the Whitehurst case or the Todd Road incident defeat a people's comfort and feeling of belonging. In the nation's inner cities, black police establishments have burned down entire blocks killing many people just to prove a point! Such was the case with the MOVE organization. The Black Panther Party headquarters was under constant threat of being raided and seized. Such was the case with Fred Hampton, Huey Newton, Bobby Hutten and others.

A good organizer does not need to be directly impacted by the issue or be from the community who is impacted. He or she needs vision that others do not have because the environment is void of understanding of the mechanics of things. He or she should expect pushback against the vision from within the ranks. Ask Moses, he will tell you that until you build trust and acceptance, the people will question your motives, misinterpret your actions and reject your plan. But hang in there. Just as Jesus said, a man's enemy will be in his own house, an organizer must expect resistance from within the group and prepare for it by always weighing dissention against the group experience. A good organizer makes everything a matter of strategy not sincerity. When some in the organization distrust the leadership in the beginning or disagree with the core values of the organization, they are admitting their need for the organization. A community organizer must say: 'If the will to organize had been present before me, it would have manifested before I showed up." Yet it remains

CHAPTER 1: What Do We Want?

to some an unreasonable and unforeseen necessity that black people actually must be prepared to assume the very responsibilities that they claim white people have forfeited. In other words, the first order of business might be to get some dirty cops fired and prosecuted, but the next day, they must be replaced with God-fearing, honest, fair and well-trained police officers. While leaving the dirty cops out to dry, a community group might serve as a liaison between the good police officers who feel outnumbered and the public schools from where the new generation of socially conscious cops will emerge. Escorting good police officers to schools to build public trust is a good public relations move. A community organization needs cops on their side. An entire prison reform movement called Free Alabama started with inmates who have, with the help of prison guards, been able to video their experiences and produce a documentary. So the community organization must be prepared to address cadets at the academy, the city council, the school board and perhaps the Fraternal Order of Police.

Sometimes, seemingly small victories have major implications and it is for this reason that a community group must pick its battles wisely. I had one friend who was an organizer in the mid-west. He was fighting urban renewal and organized some brothers to protest at a construction site. He was also going to call the construction company out on not hiring black men for projects taking place in the hood. I encouraged him not to protest but instead, bring the guys to the work site with resumes for hiring. He did so and several of the guys got hired on at a darn good pay scale. He never bothered to ask if the guys had skills which they all did and he became a go-to-guy for getting gigs. This organizer got a notch in his belt by a chance visit I made to pick up a relative of my wife from Kansas City.

When communities throughout the country begin to push for change in city hall, the ultimate end will be the United Nations. However, let this be the natural evolutionary nature of resistance efforts rather than a defined a goal. Community organizing does not have to be revolutionary because it is necessary for accomplishing goals feasible to the people. During the 60s, local issues like the death of Jimmie Lee Jackson in Marion, Alabama morphed into a march to Montgomery and then Washington which changed little back Marion. The death of Sammy Young mobilized the college student movement but it did not change things in Tuskegee where the murder happened. The historic battle between oppressor and oppressed in small towns of Alabama and abroad have been personified by city police chiefs like Bull Conner and Jim Clarke and the scenes which shocked the world like the scenes on the Edmund Pettis Bridge or the burning bus in Anniston, Alabama or the bombed church in Birmingham. All of the atrocities committed in the global military conflicts cannot touch the images on the Edmund Pettis Bridge or the bloody ambush of SNCC workers in Montgomery! Many people were arrested on the buses in Montgomery, but everybody knows Rosa Parks! Many people were killed by racist mobs, but Viola Liuzzo's name is preeminent. Thousands of people have been lynched but we remember Emmett Till. We need not have many casualties but the examples we do use must capture the essence of the people and not its glamour. We will discuss the critical error in choosing Rosa Parks for the face of the boycott over Claudette Colvin at another time.

Know Who To Trust

The Apostle Paul said that our fight is not with people but the hegemony; or the bastions of organized power in high places. He called them principalities. These hidden places are the philanthropic organizations like the Elks, Shriners, Knights of Columbus, the masons, the fraternities and sororities and the civil rights organizations like the NAACP. The "good" middle class folks who claim to be for the people and attend the galas and protests but in secret betray the people with their silence and inaction. Believe it or not Martin Luther King could have played it safe and remained apart of the compromised, sanitized and inoculated black middle class, but he chose to suffer as Moses and the Apostle did. His call to consciousness sent him to Ghana to Asia, to Vietnam and into the inner cities. He became a man of the people by adopting the cause of the poor. It became about more than dignity, it became about survival. Yet the black middle class is more about status and those with no material interest in anti-poverty outcome do not make good allies. Paul Robeson and W.E.B. Du Bois found this out the hard way, having gained little material momentum by courting the elites of society for assisting in helping poor Negroes. Marcus Garvey had no stock in the Negro elite because he believed them to be too close to the ones he was organizing against. Behind the tear gas, riot gear and armored vehicles is a man or women in a suit who is wishing that the mob not show up on voting day or at the city council meeting. I bet you, had it not been for the local efforts to organize after the death of George Floyd, the city officials would have made no attempt to get to the truth. However, when black folks burned a few buildings down and took to the streets Confederate flags came down. Social justice themes painted the television screens, and adorned the uniforms of professional athletes. Ball teams changed their names and the ethos of the corporate world adjusted with breakneck speed to the winds of pressure. Yet Negro elite will put on BLM and wear t-shirts saying "I Can't Breathe" and in the same day refuse to give their people the assistance that they REALLY need. President Barack Obama is hated for a lot of reasons. but his grassroots organizing was a serious threat. He was not an elitist nor did he come up through the traditional black ranks, so the power base never saw him coming. Yet even he defied his grassroots in many ways especially, when it came to United States foreign policy and the use military police surveillance techniques. We have former President Obama and his *Military Authorization Act* to thank for making the deployment of federal troops for local crisis such as the one fabricated by the White House to deploy federal troops to stop protesters. James Farmer in his book *Rising Tide of Black Resistance*, stated that the police became paramilitary in appearance and practice to stop the same actions in America that were taking place by the apartheid forces in South Africa. We can go a step further: the police are present now in military fashion to ensure that the American Revolution remains unfinished. The body armor, snipers, assault weapons, tear gas, armored vehicles, counter intelligence measures, helicopters and shot spotter technology while tested during criminal investigations, are employed to stop revolts and rebellions of the people when they rise against corruption. There is no history in America of black people ever fighting the police unless provoked by some miscarriage of justice on their part. Because of this, those trained in urban intelligence can predict the various forms of responses to public crises and will have already made preparation for it. Police might even preempt social unrest to misdirect others into following false altercations with police. However, what is not predicted nor expected is a "peace time" proactive organized community whose primary objective is to replace the current decision makers with themselves.

When A Swamp is Drained the Critters Come to the Front Door and Demand Entrance

President Trump ran his camping on, among other things, the promise to drain the swamp. Yet, what does a city slicker know about a swamp? A swamp or a wet land, depending on your perspective is a critical part of the ecosystem. Every animal whose habitat is a swamp including infectious diseases are at home there and great lengths go to protect swamps. Yet when a swamp is drained, the animals have nowhere to go but in the yards of people. America as a republic was not set up to accommodate so-called movements, factions or mob rule like what we saw in D.C. during the botched virtual insurrection. At the beginning, it was trying to do away with the need for such by vesting individuals with rights and by creating a pronounced separation of power. Our nation is one of individuals and the Republic protects the rights of individuals and not groups. However, when groups like the KKK and the white's citizens council organize to undermine the rights of groups, organizing as a counter moral imperative emerges. Black people organize against white supremacy. Yet those who sponsor racism and Jim Crowism are notoriously violent and throw out the Constitution, the Bible and decency to obtain their goal of power and control. The founding fathers like Alexander Hamilton stated emphatically that the only remedy for local tyranny is a change of men, meaning that an organized community does not wage an illegal take over: they work through the regular apparatus for change—which is a fair election. It is for this reason that so much effort has gone into the disfranchisement, intimidation and suppression of the black vote. The battle then and the battle now is at the courthouse where black people had to face constant intimidation and threat. Blacks were lynched or lost their jobs and homes because they registered to vote. The civil rights foot soldiers would sing the song: "Ain't gone let nobody turn us around!" This is too compromising when it comes to community organizing by today's standard. We now say: "Ain't gone let no body push us around." Someone trying to prevent a black person from voting in today's world will be met with swift and intense resistance. In community organizing today, the question is not if the community comprises of children or men, but how far are those men and women willing to go to get what they want from government.

Violence in a republic is anti-intellectual and, by nature, seditious and barbaric. Yet today, those who feel their power threatened seek to bear arms to impose intentions that cannot be enacted through conventional means. White supremacists are not organizing because black people pose a threat to them, but because their "way of life" as being a bully and a dominator is threatened. Equality to them is an insult and so many things are done to keep people in their place or class. They are afraid because the community is advancing and learning the weaknesses of their control. As Frederick Douglass stated: "At once I understood what had eluded me for so long, the white man's power to control the black man." Douglass upon learning to read as a small child understood that knowledge was the key to liberation. This is different than the civil rights movement where black people were fighting to be accepted by a failing system. Today, community organizing is focused on the reality that the system cannot be fixed and must be taken out of the hands of the powerful. This marks a growth in patriotic spirit and a refusal to see the government remain in the hands of robber barons. The community is not afraid of armed militiamen because those informed know that these guys are rebels without a cause and must use weapons that will eventually be turned on themselves by themselves. Suicide rates among police officers and the military is skyrocketing because of the pressures of maintaining illegitimate presences at home and abroad. From a community organizing stand point, I have slightly changed the song sang during the 60s to fit the purpose of the organizer: The community organizer sings this song:

> "Ain't gone let nobody push us around, push us around, push us around...we gone keep on walking, keep on talking and keep on marching and keep on fighting until we get what we want."

CHAPTER 2
The Art of Casual Complaint

The best community organizers are outsiders who work their way into a neighborhood and start asking questions that make other people uncomfortable—although many of those "*uncomfortables*" had been on the mind of many people for years. They just lacked the courage to say anything. The term *casual* means to be unassuming, and sometimes community organizers have to be low profile and inconspicuously take advantage of weaknesses in a system to get what they want from "the man". Most community organizers fail because they refuse to be creative and assume that people will just bow down to their demands. Sometimes you have to make a statement before making demands. I had been involved in local politics since my upbringing in Tuskegee wherein my dad made me campaign for Johnny Ford and then when we moved to Dadeville, my dad made me vote for Judge Sharpe. While my activities in college were apolitical, when I graduated from AUM I began to work at the U.S. Postal Service and went to law school as well. I wanted to join the postal workers union because I thought it would be fun but I was soon told that my status as a casual employee prevented me from joining. At the same time, I became president of the Christian Legal Society while in law school at Jones School of Law after the then president, who meant well, made some critical mistakes in his anti-abortion platform. I organized about 30 law students wherein I was able to invite some of the top conservative personalities to speak. Included in this cadre of speakers were then-Attorney General Jeff Session, then Chief Justice Perry Hooper Sr. and Judge Roy Moore; who at the time was mobilizing thousands to fight his Ten Commandments war in federal court. He got elected over that one issue which was a stroke of genius on his part and a great example of how local organizing morphs into political power.

While I was in law school, I worked at night at the U.S. Postal Service as a casual employee, which means that I was a temporary employee paid at the very minimum. However, the casual employees did more work than the regular employees. When I was prevented from joining the postal workers union I made the statement that shook up the Taylor Road processing facility: "I will start a casual union!" Why did I say that? Because all these old dudes started jumping my case about how casual employees had no bargaining power. While we had no bargaining power or permission to organize, we did have casual power! Everyone has potential power if properly organized. Before being hired, I went through the regular training and application process as everyone else but I was hired because the post master was a good friend of my dad. I knew nobody was going to touch me because I was "connected"—although Post Master Mitchell and I were the only two in the place who knew I was just working my way through law school. The managers and the union members on Tour 1 did not know that and considered me to be some type of trouble maker, but they did respect me very well and felt a sense of pride in my going to law school. Those old dudes were some great comrades, although they had some bad habits which I could not be involved in—at least not too much. All of the casual workers met at break and we began to spread small talk throughout the Taylor Road facility that the casuals were organizing. We would be in the break room and someone would ask: "How is the organizing going and my buddy Rick would say: "Fine, we almost there." They did not know that we were talking about the game or some other issue. Ask anyone that was there at the time, some are still living and laugh at me to this day but we formed a makeshift organization which got us better treatment from the union workers and the management. Community organizing like union organizing must be strategic. One of the things we did as mail handlers was to request to be placed on the slide, which was the main artery for mail entering the facility. With all casual workers on the slide we could control the pace of the mail flow for the entire facility. None of the old dudes wanted to work the slide because it was work! I would request to work *the hole* on the slide which was the point that all conveyor belts merged and the mail would be sorted by one person to the various routes. One night we sped the distribution of mail so fast that the belt kept jamming and being overrun with mail. The old dudes could not unload the trucks fast enough which made them look bad as well. The old union workers who were accustomed to taking their time in getting the job done were pissed for real because they actually could not keep up with the bags coming to the docks for delivery. The folks on the LSM machines were not accustomed to all these trays of mail coming at one time and management noticed that production was up considerably by our actions so they were amused and happy. They could not pay us anything more because our pay was at a set rate by the upper level people but they could give us the schedules we wanted, the days off we wanted and the shifts and job assignments we wanted and the union said nothing because they did not want to work at the speed in which we were putting out. We saying "give us what we want or else this entire belt is going to shut down and yall are going to have to do some real work!" We started getting treated much better because we did what others did not want to do and we did it better. The nature of organizing is not to make friends but to get what you want and sometimes things have to be shaken up a bit! Sometimes making the right people uncomfortable is all it takes to get things done.

Cutting My Teeth

I learned from the labor movement about power: not so much black power but organized efforts to obtain a group interest. I did not come up in any of the traditional black political organizations at the beginning of my career and I remain aloof from them to this day. I started with the AFL-CIO back in the early 90's when I began working at Alabama State University. I was not mingling with the local black power structure but was making my way up the union latter under the leadership of Dr. Nora Lawson of AFT, and Pete Wellington of the CALC. Then I met Stewart Burkhalter, Billy Tindle and the rest of the boys at the state AFL-CIO and the rest was history. A major ally in the labor movement was my friend Willie who I befriended at the Post Office. He was one of the members that pushed for me to be admitted to the postal workers union but as we said that was impossible. The labor unions organized locally to assist in the defeat of Mayor Emory Folmer and the election of Bobby Bright. We also saw a shift on the City Council and we negotiated a raise of faculty and staff at Alabama State University. I joined the Central Alabama Labor Council and I was elected Vice President of COPE for the American Federation of Teachers local chapter at Alabama State University. I was joined with union workers from various locals from around the city and then in the state. I interacted with workers from Fort Payne to the Port of Mobile and had the heads-up on a lot of things taking place in the south. I started receiving a lot of benefits such as free tickets to this and invitations to that. We strengthened the local police and Fire fighters union and rebuilt the A. Phillip Randolph Institute all under the nose of Mayor Emory Folmor; who was like a Pharaoh of sorts. I was also able to give a major address before the State AFL-CIO Convention—which was a highlight of my career. I will never forget that day. I travelled the country and learned union organizing and participated in some demonstrations as well. I learned that people were afraid of the union and in Montgomery they were terrified to the point that Mayor Folmer went through some extensive means to accomplish his ends. Montgomery had been successful at union busting up until this time because the union's effort was not very strong, and although we do not have collective bargaining in the state, we did have a strong parking lot demeanor! The city had done everything to keep union jobs away from Montgomery because the local mafia did not want anyone closing in on their racket. Yet we took these gangsters on some of us not knowing that we were becoming what we were fighting. Whatever we could not settle in the board room, we would settle in the parking lot! While I was at Alabama State University and somewhat shielded from the white backlash as we took on city hall, I was not prepared for the feedback that I and several of the members of the young Democrats got from the established black business community, black gangsters and the black clergy who were all overwhelmingly pro-Folmer. This man seemed to have everybody in his pocket and none of the black established politicians would cross him. But we did and it paid off for us. We went door to door and registered an unusually large number of new voters which always spells defeat for an incumbent. We also got support from private persons and then from the organized workers at the state, county and city level. None were open in their endorsements but secretly voted for us. We snuck around and put Bobby Bright stickers on city vehicles and put yard signs at the residents of loyal Fomler voters! We were loud, obnoxious and very aggressive and saw the dynasty fold. I never forget when some organizers and I met with some cops after hours to try and get some valuable intel. They looked me in the eye and basically said: "Boy I hope you are right because if we go out on a limb for you and we lose, my family does not eat and I will have to leave town." I was so confident that I assured these guys that he would get his raise and promotion if he supported us and we made good on it! We were successful because we had **TACK**. The people TRUSTED us; they ACCEPTED us, we were CONSISTANT in our speech and actions and we were the KNOWLEDGE source for building the vision. The reason why I am sure that mayors must be held accountable is because not soon after Bobby Bright was elected, our relationship with him went south and a lot of our alliances in city hall dissolved or transformed; as well they should have done. But it was a natural death. The crew ended up opposing Bobby Bright and getting into disagreements with him but I had gotten out by then. However, many of the foot soldiers took jobs in the local and state government and I went to become an in house lawyer for the most powerful special interest group in Alabama history if not the entire country when it comes to state politics: The Alabama Education Association.

The AEA and The ADC

Dr. Paul Hubbard and Dr. Joe Reed are the twin towers of political organizing. They both began locally, Dr. Hubbard in Walker County and Dr. Reed on the campus of Alabama State College and in the city of Montgomery. Dr. Reed got his start as a student at the college and worked his way up to become the chairman of the board of trustees. While coming from different sides of the track, they both knew their communities well and were able to successfully merge their respective teacher organizations to create a superpower in regional politics. These two men had **TACK**; the **trust** of the people; **acceptance** of the people, they were **consistent** in what they said and they had superior **knowledge** of the subject matters at hand. Dr. Hubbard knew the white citizenry and they trusted him and Dr. Reed through the Alabama Democratic Conference had his pulse on every election that involved black candidates and voters. Together they built an empire that cornered Alabama politics for decades. The AEA got superintendents, legislators, school board members and governors hired and fired, elected and defeated and basically controlled the entire function of state government. They got AEA week or Spring Break for the teachers, and created the Education Trust fund and a retirement system for teachers which better ensured that politics could not be played with public education. They had lobbyists, lawyers, activists, field staff and an organized membership of thousands which put the clamps on local politics. Dr. Reed had tapped me to be his legal assistant and it was my pleasure. My corner office overlooked Dexter King Memorial Baptist Church and right up the street was the State Capital. The glare from the marble steps would gleam through my window so brightly I would have to close the blinds. Everybody who was somebody came to the 3rd floor of our building to ask favors and kiss the ring. I learned that, at some point, the terms *Republican* and *Democrat* become irrelevant and that politics is about winning before the battle begins and things simply play themselves out in the legislature. I learned from Dr. Reed and Hubbard that planning is sometimes an all night and weekend labor of love. It is always taking place and involves arriving early and leaving late. Did I mention that the AEA had its own polling agency which on the eve of the American Idol climax sent hundreds of calls into the show to get Ruben Studdard picked? Politics involves constant communication and verification of facts. It involves taking darn good care of your friends and even feeding your enemies when they need help. But the end game is power and winning and, to win, planning must take place. AEA had some of the most effective people doing what they did best and everybody respected them. All I had to say was that I am with AEA and doors opened up. Dr. Reed, while being the chairman of the Alabama Democratic Committee and Alabama Executive Committee, had some of the top lawyers in the nation on his legal team and my relationship with most of them are still solid. Dr. Reed knew more law than any lawyer and his battle wounds earned him a right to speak whenever and wherever he chose. But he made a lot of sense and he is the most admired man in my life except for my dad. He had a lot of enemies as well, mostly because he did not share power. What impressed me about Dr. Reed also was his willingness to hear my opinion, no matter how off base it might have been. While deliberating with other lawyers over some issue in his office, he would ask me my opinion and he would always say: "Make your point" or "Don't abandon your point!" He would almost get upset with me when I didn't support my own argument when challenged. He taught me not to diminish or under estimate the contribution someone could make even if they were the least in the group. I really had no business being there because I was not a lawyer (having not passed the bar at that time), but they made me feel like I was an expert and that has paid off to this day in the form of speaking engagements and invitations to the decision making table at various levels and most importantly: respect. What impressed me about these legal giants was how humble and willing they were to listen to me, a kid who had not practiced a lick of law in my life, but I knew what I knew. The lobbyists were nice and I eventually became one myself. The office was a home away from home. We had a workout facility and a room with televisions. On election night we would have hundreds of people come through and we would entertain them and eat all night long. Sometimes you have to be the first get to the office and the last to leave. I tell people don't ever be in a hurry to leave because the best conversations take place after 5. We would sit up in someone's office for hours talking about cases and judges and clients. I learned so much while at AEA! I have seen legislators spend hours filibustering on the floor against some AEA bill only to turn around and come to the 3rd floor and ask for money. While at AEA, I learned that planning was about power! I got a chance to witness so much and most impressive of all was the art of compromise when planning legislation. However, the fact that my window faced the capital was symbolic, because my desire and my fate would take me up Goat Hill to the cat bird seat of Alabama politics. My next move would put me at ground zero of Alabama politics.

As I sat in my office at AEA I learned that I could not function in an office environment, tied to an office chair all day. Also, some entanglements that my family had with Dr. Reed made my presence at AEA kind of suspect because my mom was the Vice President of Alabama State University where Dr. Reed was chair of the board of Trustees. I was planning to go to seminary anyway, but for some reason the capital was calling me and I would soon find out why. I would think: "I wonder what it is like working up there?" I wanted to be out and among people and not end up stuck in an office working on cases and answering the phone, although it was one heck of a job which I was extremely grateful to this day.

The State Capital is Haunted!

I was fortunate enough to sit and learn so much at AEA and although the job was mammoth, fate would soon take me to the State Capital under the leadership of Nancey Worley who was elected Secretary of State for Alabama. I also was called to Pastor Pilgrim Rest Baptist Church in Greenville, Alabama. So my community organizing served to help with the administration at the Capital as well as the church. I was a good asset to the office because I had already made my rounds in the state through my preaching, the labor unions and AEA. I had met Nancey when she was President of AEA's membership and the same day I decided to leave AEA, she asked me to work for her. While with the Secretary of State, I served as lobbyist and interim director of elections for the state which was right in line with my desire to get more experience in how decisions are made in government. The first full day on the job, I stayed in the office until almost midnight assisting the staff attorney Trey Grainger in writing the regulations which would bring the State of Alabama into conformity with the newly enacted federal Help America Vote Act or HAVA. I know what downtown Montgomery looks like at the wee hours of the morning. This assignment was the most challenging I'd had yet, but I enjoyed all of the drama and chaos that came with it. I had never seen so many casualties of war than during this administration, and enemies were flying from all angles—the most damaging coming from inside the office. I travelled all over the state again, visiting every courthouse in the state and getting a chance to meet the probate judges, sheriffs, voting registrars and city clerks. Community organizers should know that the main reason why local government is screwed up is because there is no training associated with taking office nor is it required that the candidate know what he or she is doing. For example, voting registrars were selected because of their connections and most of them had no idea what they were doing and my

CHAPTER 2: The Art of Casual Complaint

office's meddling made matters worse. It is hard to organize around inadequate disorganized government but it is not the fault of the good people in the positions more so than it is with those elected officials who benefit from the chaos. I got to know the local people and have developed relationships with a lot of them that last to this day. I have had to count petition signatures of hundreds of people at a time and stay up all night manning phones on election night. We even had to be in the office during a hurricane because an election deadline was held on the same day. When I say all politics are local, I mean it. Despite the governor's races and the fierce legislative battles, the time I feared for my life was when I and other office colleagues were called upon to travel to a small town somewhere to mediate an issue between candidates running for county bird watcher, or city dog catcher and butterfly counter! Those local fights are the worst, and yes, people get seriously hurt over these small town elections. My former boss and mentor Dr. Reed would always say: "If you don't know people you are going to fail!" A good community organizer develops an intuition about people that you better not betray. Community organizers must learn the personality of the people with whom he or she is going to work and if you do not betray what you feel about a person, you can work with them without them ever hurting or disappointing you. I heard Jerome Gray, Dr Reed's field director at ADC, say "Never let a hungry man carry your lunch." When you are honest with what you feel about a person's character and you can keep it to yourself, it is then that you can discern the best methods to approach getting things done.

The AFl-CIO, The NSC and Jerome Gray

Jerome Gray is one of the best field organizers I have ever met. His primary role was to be field director for the Alabama Democratic Conference which was headed up by my former boss, Dr. Reed. Although my former boss was a city council person in Montgomery for many years, he was the head of a state organization as then Mayor Emory Folmer was for the Republican Party. Mr. Gray has mentored countless numbers of young people and has been unselfish in his desire to see change. He has served on countless boards and delegations and has been at the epicenter of Alabama and national politics. I can say that if there was no Jerome Gray there would be no Robert White because he found me and took me under his wing. I cut my teeth in community organizing with the American Federation of Teachers which is a part of the American Federation of Labor-Union of Industrial Organizations. Although I was established with the AFL-CIO, I had no dealings with local black politicians, the Young Democrats or local black political organizations. I was introduced to Jerome Gray by Pete Wellington, who was president of the Central Alabama Labor Council and we immediately struck up a friendship. Pete was also one heck of a community and union organizer. Pete was a white guy who was very jolly and after he got to know me, we developed a good working relationship. Pete lived in Titus, Alabama and had people's respect when it came to local politics, particularly because he'd been fire fighter for some years. Pete introduced me to Jerome and it was Jerome that introduced me to Rev. James Orange and Rev. Andrew Young. I will never forget when I was called into a meeting and these guys were sitting at the table. These civil rights heroes were very nice to me and I was amazed at the sit down time that Jerome allowed me to have with them whenever they were in town. Jerome and Dr. Reed were responsible for getting almost all of the black candidates elected and their organization eventually split into two groups; the other group being the New South Coalition (NSC) which was established by then Senator Hank Sanders, his wife Faya Rose Ture and others. At this point, it is important to state that there are different forms of community organizing. The NSC comprised of several local black belt groups that took matters into their own hands, sometimes by protesting and other times by more theatrical forms of disobedience like singing, chants, improving the appearance of public property, etc. They defend high and low profile clients and also officiate the historic Bloody Sunday Selma Jubilee festivities. I am as indebted to Hank and Faya as I am to Dr. Reed although these giants split from each other and remained somewhat antagonistic at times. The New South Coalition consists of several local Black Belt groups. The Save Ourselves Organization, the 21st Century Youth Leadership Core and the Africa 360 project are some of the organizations that have been founded under their auspices. The interesting thing about the New South Coalition is its power base which is, interestingly, not very strong in local Selma politics, but resounding outside the city of Selma and in the rural of the Black Belt. Selma is a tough city in which to organize because of the impoverished black residents who seem to be beholden to local white influence, although the numbers of whites is diminishing considerably.

A community organizer's good name rests on their affiliation and sometimes affiliations can hinder o make problematic the advancement of a group. In politics and community organizing, loyalty is important. Since AEA took the chance and hired me I feel loyal to that culture whether they are in power of not. We always say "you don't drop old friends to make new ones." And I have been able to remain loyal to my former bosses while at the same time making meaningful and profitable relationships with a lot of other people. I have been approached to deliver messages to my former boss and even have been tapped to call meetings which amounted to little or nothing. My bosses have always been polarizing but maintain clear lines of communication which are critical. Keep your alliances fresh and clean and flee from even the appearance of evil! However, I know when to pick sides and it has always been with my former boss. I have learned when someone is clear about his or her intentions and associations and does not try to be opportunistic, people will respect them. I say "If one waits for the right time rather than jumping at the fool's gold, things will come to you without having to burn a bridge." There were times when a lot of people went against my bosses like Dr. Reed, Mayor Johnny Ford, Madam Secretary Worley or former Senator Hank Sanders. But my mom and dad always taught me to be loyal to my bosses and never turn on them. That teaching has stuck with me and I have had to live it. When they win, they always remember me in some way and when they lose, I contact them. Not everyone can say this, and my experience is not typical. I know that, and it is for this reason that the bulk of my presentation on TACK is about the science of organizing and not my own personal experience which is not transferable to others. I remember when I worked at AEA and my friend, former Senator and now President of Alabama State University, Quinton Ross was running against my boss for State Senate, I had no problem remaining loyal to my boss. When things got heated between him and Quinton, I came to his office and told him that he had nothing to worry about when it came to me and that I was dedicated to him. I knew he trusted me because he discussed campaign secrets with me in the office knowing that Quinton and I were close. I think he appreciated me coming to him; especially when others were jumping ship so to speak. But because I had never been fully apart of the Young Democrats who had autonomy to act as they saw fit, I did not have the attachment to the group as others did and because I worked for AEA, I had little leisure. Affiliation is a big deal in organizing and each organization has its own ethos and pathos.

The election of President Barak Obama was the single greatest tragedy for Alabama politics because it polarized an entire state and threw it out of kilter. The AFL-CIO was majority white working class people who had a lot of organizing power; especially in the northern part of the state. However, they were overwhelmingly Democrat and would work with you very well although some of them were closet racists. Blacks and whites were in the same party and as dysfunctional as they were, the election of Democratic governors and legislators was a sure thing until the race card became the trump card! I helped organize white people in

CHAPTER 2: The Art of Casual Complaint

Calhoun and Etowah County and they listened to me, made me dinner and even let me rest on their front porch. There was no "make American great again" because we were fighting a common enemy, which was management. But when President Obama got in office, community organizing died and this racist, illogical, unhealthy, unscientific spirit consumed politics, and man, was it a mighty fall. Everything AEA had spent years building collapsed and it was partly due to the National Education Association's (NEA) obsession with a left wing agenda, which Dr. Hubbert and Dr. Reed had refrained from endorsing. Political and community organizing must be proactive and this did not jibe with the overwhelmingly reactive nature of the NEA. Sadly, we saw it coming, and the AEA was defanged by its own national affiliate. The powerhouse was gone and the Obama administration made little or no effort in helping to restore supremacy—even allowing the Holder v. Shelby County case to fall through the cracks, which gutted the Voting Rights Act. At the same time that the Voting Rights Act was nullified, in a contradiction of logic and rationality, the Republicans passed a voter ID bill which further hindered minority voters. While Jerome was as happy as ever with the notion of having a black president, other black leaders like then Rep. Alvin Holmes and John Knight were concerned that an Obama win would piss white folks off in the south, and they were right. But it was Jerome that predicted that Barak Obama would become president. Jerome knew every back road and knew the "who's who" among Alabama and national politics and Robert Smith, a good friend and proficient assistant in his own right, kept all loose ends covered. These guys knew their stuff, having filed several successful lawsuits and having enacted many policy changes that helped a lot of black people. Yet Jerome and Dr. Reed were from a small country town in Conecuh County Alabama. It seems that small towns produce the biggest influential figures in Alabama politics which brings us again to the priority of local community organizing. As former legislator Steve Flowers would say: Alabama governor's races are won and lost at the feed store. While Mr. Gray was active, he had what it took to be, for the Alabama Democratic Conference, what was necessary. He has nurtured so many young politicians and there are so many people who owe their careers to Jerome.

An organizer has to use the environment to his or her advantage. Being in the AFL-CIO gave me statewide connections and teaching at the university gave me access to hundreds of students. I had influence, access and negotiation leverage, and I used them to the advantage of the teachers and support workers at the school. Yet I had no power. Soon, I was introduced to the local political hierarchy and with my state connections, money came into my pocket from many sources and I was able to work a short stint of success into a lifelong career. Jerome worked it for me to receive money to fund political activities and the AFL-CIO followed. So I had a checkbook and a nice flow of funds which I distributed very liberally. I will never forget that I was summoned to a meeting of local politicians who all asked me for money. I was so liberal with it, giving them more than they asked. That let them know that I could not be bought. In fact, Rob and I kept none of it, so no one could say we were hungry or sloppy, not that anybody cared, but we would have fallen into the category of people that could not be trusted and there were enough of those types. To gain trust, a community organizer must not be a thief or crook. Even the real crooks will respect you if you are not one of them. They might not invite you to steal with them, but when they need someone honest, they will call you and it's all good and legal because they know you don't do illegal stuff. While at the elections division for the Secretary of State's office, I saw so many black politicians (and white ones too) go to jail for stealing from their own campaigns, but how many lobbyists have gone to jail? My former boss Madam Secretary got arrested for campaign activities as did my friend President Quinton Ross when he was state senator. In Quinton's case, I thought it was wrong to wiretap during a campaign season because the information could easily be compromised or used for political purposes. My friends was arrested at early morning at home jailed and intensely prosecuted before being found not guilty. It was all a political tactic to limit his political power but those who tried to take him got took out by the same or similar circumstances. God don't like ugly and if you dig a ditch for others be prepared to fall into it. That's what they do. They get you wrapped up in court so you lose your mind along with your family and your money. Even if you are successful, you are out of hundreds of thousands of dollars! A community organizer must refrain from lying or stealing so no one can bring to question their integrity. However, a community organizer is not a sinless messiah and must show some sign of weakness or a proclivity so that others will not think he or she is trying to be an elitist or moralist. A community organizer is not a religious leader but is a man or woman of the people, a human being like those he or she has come to help.

Political advocacy deals with raising issues but getting legislation passed or getting candidates elected is called political action which has strict laws assigned to this activity. Political organizing and community organizing is not the same thing. Community organizing focuses on issues while political campaigns focus on individual personalities. When Jerome introduced me to Dr. Reed, I was hired to assist him in organizing his campaign for re-election on the city council which included an intense effort on the campus. Dr. Reed did not need my expertise, but he did need my leg work and influence at ASU to get students out to vote. I was also on the Bobby Bright campaign as well. I set up a debate between he and the opposition candidate Tracy Larkin, who had been my dad's DJ when he owned night clubs in Tuskegee. So it felt weird opposing my dad's friend, but it was all good. I was working for Bobby Bright and I had no idea what we were getting into with trying to dethrone Mayor Emory Folmer. In dealing with Bobby Bright, I saw just why it so hard to organize the community to better the community, because Emory Folmer was paying so many black people to work for him. This included preachers, teachers, gangsters and the like. It is for this reason that I say the ultimate enemy is city hall, because a mayor controls everything. I could do community organizing for Bobby Bright, but not for Dr. Reed because of the personality and trends in political sentiment toward establishment candidates. I was successful with Bright but Dr. Reed lost his city council seat at the same time that Emory Folmer lost his mayoral seat. Yet, ASU had the highest voter turnout in decades and the energy on the campus was at an all-time high. Later, with Gore/Bush, an entirely new form or organizing had to occur, especially when the PAC to PAC transfer prohibitions took effect. What distinguished Bobby Bright from Dr. Reed was a lot of factors but the misinterpretation of political power with community sentiment is a major contributor. A person with political power might lose in the realm of public opinion. It is at this point that community organization becomes critical because it is the organization that sets the priorities and not the political power of any one individual.

Know When to Change Directions

I got out of organized labor when it got a little messy, but I understood power from a dynamic that my other African American colleagues had not. I was moving up the ranks with unions and I was slipping into an area that was not healthy so I backed off before I got too deep. Everybody seems to understand when I back off that I have gone as far as my conscience would let me. Community organizers have to have influence, money and muscle and sometimes you have to flex it, but there are limits. One has to spot when things are taking a turn toward an unintended direction, and bow out with dignity. Sometimes, the greater your success, the higher the stakes next time around. However, to maintain one's integrity, although sometimes you have to make threats and make good on them, never ever go to bed with the people that you might have to challenge. Politically speaking, the best way to neutralize an opponent is to pay their debts for them. This is where political action (power) and specifically Political Action Committees (PACs) come in because the purpose of election laws is to provide legal means of contributing to a campaign or legislative action. My mentor would always say "If you try to get rich while you are an elected official, you are going to jail." If you have money, you can turn your enemies into your friends by paying their election debts. I do not give to campaigns until after the election is over. Help candidates pay their debts and that way—win or lose—you got them owing you. People will respect you if you can hurt them politically so be prepared to get your hands dirty as you push for what you want.

Rural Church Organizing

When I left AEA, the same day I was hired at the Secretary of State's Office, I was called to be the pastor of Pilgrim Rest Baptist Church in Greenville, Alabama. They were some good people, but the church organization was personality based—as are most churches. Country folks are different from others in that they have an intuition and a discernment that is not modern but has developed over years of experience. An incoming preacher needs to know where the bastion of power is in the church and who the main brokers of that power are. Typically the person who has the authority to change the thermostat without being asked is the boss. The one who speaks last or not at all is the house dog and these people are not going to just surrender their position and authority and preeminence to a new pastor until trust can be earned. My ministry hinged on the two groups that became the generating culture in the church: the youth and the mothers of the church. Those already in power in the church are also propped up by the community power dynamic, which is to say that many of those deacons who run the church have support of the local white hegemony. I wondered why, when a church has a dispute with a pastor, the sheriff is called and the pastor is escorted out and not the trouble making members. It is because the local banks persuade churches to take out loans and they become the trustee of the churches finances. If a preacher gets out of line, the deacons are the ones whose name is on the note so they call the shots. Many of my pastor friends would show up at church only for their key to not work. This meant that while he was at home, the church folks called a meeting and voted him out. People always asked me why I never ran for public office, and it was because I was elected every Monday morning! I have one friend that outlasted me in the ministry and has survived countless votes of no confidence partly because they did not like the changes he was bringing to the table.

When I first became pastor, I had to earn the **trust** of the church and then the entire community. You know people begin to trust you when they allow you into their personal lives. You gain **acceptance** when you are invited to events like children's birthday parties, graduations, weddings and funerals. You experience the best and worst of times with people and they begin to take risks for you. When you come from another place, your ideas distinguish you from people who have lived there for long periods of time and you become a **knowledge** source for them. The longer you remain, your consistency of personality and temperament builds your relationship to the point that they stop watching you and analyzing you to the point of inactivity. The key to longevity in a rural church is to not get too comfortable and constantly keep the people challenged beyond their experiences. Do things out of the ordinary and get in good with the mothers of the church and the community leaders. Visit them and ask their opinion. Ask the youth their opinion and ask the deacons their opinion. I encouraged dialogue amongst members and even instigated conversations outside the church. As long as the people knew that you were not threatened by their conversation and that they wouldn't be threatened for stating their opinion, the more clear communication our mutual communication became. We did not argue and we did not have business meetings because any member at any time could ask a trustee to see the financial records of the church. I did not steal any of their money, nor did I sleep with any of their women. I kept my life open and examinable and sometimes I gave my entire check back to the church. When we did have church meetings, I let the people make the decisions and the vote had to be at least 90% in favor of what we needed to do. I would sometimes even call for another vote because the margin of yeas and nays was too close. I represented them with class and the church grew. I did not keep the checkbook but I stood in line to pick up my check just like the lady that cleaned the church. Over time, power positions in the church became tenuous and bothersome to the established vestiges of church power, and they resigned to the silent seats, but still tried walking the fence to stay close enough to know what is going on but far away to not be held accountable or responsible for anything. A lot of black church activities have been shaped by white supremacy including when we have revival, how we count money and even which Sundays we worship.

A community leader must challenge the local hegemony. The fear-brokers in the community must be faced or confronted with boldness. Again, if the people had balls, it would have shown up before you got there. While at Pilgrim Rest, I was reminded by the elders of the church that white people would barge in on worship service and snatch people up to come and lay by their crops. After hearing this, I said one day in my sermon: "If any white man steps foot in here to get any of you out to work in the fields, they are leaving in a stretcher!" This put all those men in the church in a very peculiar position because basically I was saying: "Y'all are not men for letting white folks come in your place and make you do anything. An outsider is here and yaall might as well sit down." This got a lot of amens from the women folk and the radicals in the congregation who had been thinking it but had no opportunity to say it. A community man or woman says what the people are thinking! While at Pilgrim Rest, my wife, staff and I made major inroads toward uniting Greenville, which was split along all type of lines. I made pastors like me get along with each other outside of the association lines, and gave tokens of appreciation and good will. Because I worked at the Capitol, I was very familiar with the elected officials in the area who called on me from time to time for help. We got people out of jail and helped them during some very rough times. The passing of loved ones, family reunions, graduations, field trips and community events were all a part of the job, but the home cook meals and relaxing times on the porch with a glass of lemonade were the best. We got a lot of stuff done because they trusted my wife and I. They accepted us into their culture and we were consistent in our treatment of them. Finally, we remained the primary source of information for many of them regarding things outside of their experience. Even now, many of the people who were at Pilgrim Rest support our current ministry. We stayed in Greenville for 11 years and I enjoyed every minute of it, I learned a lot from the people there and I would hope that a surge in black political activity can be traced back to our ministry which exposed the church to all types of personalities. However, I never made any bones about being an outsider and the significant sacrifice my family was making to help them.

What Is Power?

Like I said above, I had a lot working for me when I was with the unions but I had no power outside of my persuasion. Power is the ability to protect, pursue and advance one's elf interest and the Or Else Factor: that means having bargaining power is critical to maintain power. A good community organizer does not want the powers that be to fall or fail. They simply want the powers to give them what they want without having to sell their soul in the process! As Ayn Rand says: there is a certain virtue in being selfish. This means that it's ok to have ideas, ambitions, desires, and objectives that you would like to reach. However, altruists believe these things should go to others before one's self. If a person wishes to sacrifice for the sake of others that is ok, but no one should be forced to do it—especially if the benefactors feel entitled to the hard work of others. A republic leaves every man to his own abilities and his own thoughts as the main means of producing his way in life. However, we are also in a democracy, meaning that those who possess the same interests tend to unite into factions in the hopes of getting what they want out of life even if it means trampling on the rights of others. This makes for a mob mentality, and it is from democracy that marches and protests come. Power does not need to march or perform open displays of aggression. If you want to know how power works, look to the powerful, who rule by stealth, deception, perception, logic and proactive measures. The powerful are never reacting to others; they force others to react to them. According to Frederick Douglass "Power concedes nothing without demand." When those who stand to lose or obtain the same things unite, the interest becomes a group interest and force becomes the main tool for advancement. It is from group interests that special interest groups, issue advocacy groups, political parties and political action committees emerge. Most of your political organizing in Alabama is done based on interests and not neighborhoods; wealth and not community. The wealthy land owners, the manufacturers and the banks control everything and maintain the status quo. They do this through politics and they have lobbyists and campaign contributions to help. SNCC took on Chase Manhattan Bank and the Communities Not Prisons organization took on Regions Bank and Corecivc and won! Yet understanding the changing definitions of terms is important. This means that various groups must do the same things to compete and this is difficult because the people might not have the time or attention to have an enduring presence in the legislature. Things there might be or seem inconsequential to the life styles of many people, meaning there might not be an immediate need to monitor the legislature all the time.

When we say "community", we are not only talking about a geographical set up but a unity of interests. People can live in the same neighborhood but not have the same interests. A community exists among people who have a same standard of living. Community is about objectivity and every business or trade group has a fundamental standard of living. What is a particular community's business standard is important when measuring the amount of resistance you will receive. If you want to put a night club in a part of town, the good folks that live over there need to be in favor of it or not. Montgomery in the 70's and 80's, as conservative as it was, had many x rated movie houses and adult establishments because the community was willing to allow the two to exist together. A community organizer, to be a player on the game he or she must be on the field. But not now. Communities are comprised of like-minded or similarly situated people. The most recent community that I have learned about are people who comprise a neuro community. They use to be called retarded or autistic. Now they have lobbyists, interests, standards and policy issues that they wish to push. They have become a force with which to be reckoned! In building a community, you are building a consensus for the purpose of fulfilling a common interest. Only those impacted by the issue are a part of the community. The "Latino" or "LGBTQ" community is an organized body of people who fit that demographic or sector of the population. Sometimes issues intersect and the need for form associations emerges. An association is a confederated link between private or centralized organizations. Each organization maintains and gives up a certain amount of autonomy to be numbered together for a common purpose.

CHAPTER 3
By Power, We Get Things Done

By power, we mean the ability to get things done either through diplomacy or force. A *community* comprises of individuals who in their individual capacity comprise a minority unto themselves, but collectively they become unified in purpose, thought and action. Community organizing does not remove a king from his castle or authority from its traditional place, but seeks to use group influence to get what is best for the community–whatever that may be. A community organizer, as opposed to a self-proclaimed community activist and leader is not individualistic, dictatorial, dogmatic or ideological; which excludes many traditional positions of authority in the community from taking the lead. Some pastors might be great church organizers and awesome speakers but terrible community organizers because their religious dogma, church obligations and congregational entanglements might alienate the community. Yet a dynamic pastor like Adam Clayton Powell, Vernon Johns or Calvin Butts might be a great mobilizer in that people will come to hear their sermon or speech when it is time to act.

The Montgomery Bus Protest was started by two groups: the Women's Political Council and the Montgomery Improvement Association. After King was elected Pastor of Dexter Avenue Baptist Church, he was elected president of the MIA without him being at the meeting. As stated in the testimony of the Browder v Gayle case, the people chose King to be their spokesperson but they had no leader. One Plaintiff said: "He does not represent no one, we represent ourselves. We appointed him as our leader! After King was elected president, he left the organizing to the Montgomery Improvement Association (MIA) and the Women's Political Council (WPC) in Montgomery and as the movement expanded outside of Montgomery, he relied on the Student Non-Violent Coordinating Committee in Greensboro and Lowndes County, Alabama. King and the other preachers showed up when the television cameras were there to move the crowds to action for a specific time and place. The mass meeting came about as a climax to months of intense community organizing by nameless foot soldiers and not simply to energize people who have no agenda but to raise hell. SNCC was successful in (TACK) organizing the community because they:

1) took the time to earn the **trust** of the people;
2) were **accepted** by the people;
3) were **consistent** in their activities and
4) had **knowledge** of what needed to be done.

Also, in an organized setting, traditional authoritative figures like pastors and politicians might be uncomfortable in environments where there is an equality of ideas and free thought. Politicians might be in it purely for the votes, but not for the action. Yet a community organizer sets to reorganize the people around real, objective, material issues that can only be solved by the implementation of specific measures dictated by the group. The community organizer is not trying to create a vision or dream but a plan and blueprint that the people have agreed is necessary cause of action.

We must operate with the understanding that while he or she can do all things in Christ. They might not get the credit, but will always get the blame. An effective community organizer must know that he or she's best weapon is to remain anonymous and not have his or her name attached to any effort. Rather, it is the people who take the credit for the organization. It is an error to assume that the community is not already organized because it is very much so. It is organized into pathos; a "way of death," which suits the needs of the powers structure that is always represented in a city by city hall. City Hall is always the enemy because it sustains its power from what the Occult Technology of Power calls deception. If not checked by the people, the mayor's office breeds dope dealing, gangs, blight, sex trafficking, trash in the streets, red lining and liquor stores along with all of the economic growth and opportunity as well. It is this funky dialectic which keeps people disorientated and bewildered. City Hall creates every vice, including police brutality and domestic violence. Anyone who knows anything knows that a city is controlled by the mayor's office and trying to get city hall to change is harder than confronting Washington D.C., which is not a state but a city as well! The city is actually an extension of the mayor's character and the police force, and other auxiliaries are extensions of his or her own ego. It is this reason, Proverbs 11;10 says " When it goeth well with the righteous, the city rejoices and when the wicked perisheth, there is shouting." When a mayor is defeated, it is always an advantage however, what is not assumed is the responsibility of putting someone into office that will do what you wish.

Arnold Toynbee published a series of books on the theme A Study of History, wherein he discussed his theory of role reversal. This is his observation of how a group who is responsible for one victory, in one era, used that victory as justification to maintain power until another group removes them. Because the group who won the victory glorifies the past, they refuse to use innovation to approach new challenges and end up becoming the new oppressors. Toynbee used the Pharisees in Jesus' day as an example. The nucleus for the Pharisees was formed during the times of the Jewish struggle against the Greeks but had become a part of the hegemony under the Roman occupation. Although their history as Jewish nationalists earned them respect and honor in one generation, it did not preclude them from becoming the major source of localized oppression. They had to go, but it was like pulling teeth! A community organizer should be prepared to be opposed by the very people who were so-called change agents in the previous era. This is role reversal at its finest when the former civil rights folks use their clout to stop progress! A community organization does not wish to kill anyone or cause anyone to perish. Instead, the organizer simply applies this proverb to the political death one receives when they are defeated by the forces of righteousness. However, those who win power have to be monitored by the least of these lest those placed in power replace the tyrants whom they replaced.

Any sense of reorganization in the community draws the attention of the status quo elite who guard the hood like a hawk. It took them years to master the environment and they took drastic steps to create the current conditions. The ruling elite of a city is its lifeblood. The elite control all the incoming business and they divide up the spoils. They plan the rise and fall of communities and at their whim, and hang the life experiences of its citizens in the balance. They know where the drugs will be sold they know where the prostitution as well child trafficking will take place. They know where the secret spots will be in their preferred communities. They know when crimes occur and seek to manage the madness. Their job is to control it, manage it and facilitate it, not to stop it. Those being managed have no recourse or defense against them except but to remove them from office. Proverbs 19:4 says: "Wealth maketh many friends but the poor is separated from his neighbor." The forces that have already organized the community know the environment they have created, and they also know when something is not right. Politicians consider any independent act of organizing a threat to their political power and will either seek to stop it, slow it down so it can be controlled, co-opt it by putting their own people in, or waiting to see if it is successful and then take the credit for something they did not do. They sow the discord and the instability and profit from the black on black crime, drug addiction and 3rd world like conditions. If one were to study the way colonial powers undermine African countries, he or she would also understand how the ghettoes of America are controlled. A visit to any African or Caribbean country could lead one to conclude that the power structure in Montgomery, Selma, Birmingham, and Atlanta are handled the same as the power structures in Africa. The most elusive set involves black leaders put in puppet power to do to black people what white people used to do. Franz Fanon stated that the colonial powers learn to rule from a distance, and the greater the distance the colonial power is from the colony the more mystifying their control. It would seem that those in control are godlike or ordained to lead and rule simply because they appear to be so brilliant in their acts, which, to the oppressed seems to be impossible to defeat. This is not the case, and only community organizing can make that clear. In sporting events, each team has a game plan. In the theater, everyone has the same script. In academia everyone has basically the same text books and instruction. But in community organizing that is not the case. It is for this reason that all community organizing must be anti-status quo and overtly and secretly hostile to status quo politics. Two personalities immediately come to mind when we talk about community organizing. A. Phillip Randolph who formed the Union of Sleeping Car Porters and Paul Robeson the Council on African Affairs. In his book entitled Crisis of the Negro Intellectual, Harold Cruise analyses the reason why Randolph succeeded in his efforts while Robeson did not. Cruise basically states that Randolph sought to organize the Negro worker who had zeal and nothing to lose and everything to gain, while Robeson spent most of his time courting people who had no motive or incentive to become active—this group being the bourgeoisie class.

What Is a Community?

Our nation is divided into many subgroups, cohorts and classifications. Usually a community is comprised of those who share in a geographic area; a neighborhood and its many bodies. A community association might deal with home ownership but what about the businesses and the schools and churches that share the same land and people? What about the alumni residence and the kids that live in the neighborhood? A community is already organized, but often times it is done by preexisting circumstances. A major aspect of housing discrimination is that the communities were created by land developers in conjunction with the government to further an economic and political agenda. The goal of the community organizer is to reorganize people and relationships that have been created from reactionary causes.

Community organization—which should not to be confused with community organization(s)—typically last about five years. This observation comes from monitoring the plight of organizers as Saul Alinsky, Fanny Lou Hammer, E.D. Nixon Robert Sobukwe, Stockley Carmichael, Medgar Evers and others. Each of the persons mentioned were associated with organizations that have fallen into obscurity. Why do we know individuals and not the organizations that they created or in which they participated?

Missing from the list is Martin Luther King Jr. This is not a mistake, because those who knew him best recognize his value as a mobilizer. It was a strategy of organizations like the Southern Christian Leadership Conference to search out cities where the people were already organized. In Lowndes County, Alabama and in Mississippi, local people organized with the help of various local and national organizations. The Student Nonviolent Coordinating Committee did most of the foot work, conducted the sit-ins and voter registration drives. Their efforts in Lowndes County built a political party to offset the immoral and unresponsive Democratic Party. The organization that emerged from the local effort was the Lowndes County Freedom Organization which, after the death of Malcolm X, took root in Oakland California at Merritt College. While the preachers were organized under the SCLC, SNCC under the inspiration of Ella Baker comprised the foot soldiers of the movement. These college students came from all over, mostly from HBCUs and lent their courage and zeal to people already committed to the cause. The purpose was uniform and easy to understand: to obtain political power!

The Mystique of A Good Community Organizer: The Perpetual Outsider

A good community organizer must be sent for by the people. He or she must be invited into the community and must receive overwhelming support from the inner circle of the community culture. A culture is an environment that reproduces like kind, which means a person emerging from a culture is a representation of the whole, and not an exception to the rule. A community is best organized around the "what is" not the "what should be." A community organizer that is willing to accept the people for what they are without mandating that they change is critical because good community organizing uses the strengths and weaknesses of the community to its advantage. He or she does not seek to lead the people in a way that they know not because it makes the group dependent on the organizer. So when the organizer is killed, called to another assignment or is compromised for some reason, the organization can continue because the organizer was not necessarily a apart of the organization. For example, Bayard Rustin was the brain trust around a lot of what Martin Luther King took the credit for. Bayard Rustin was not interested in the lime light but he was totally committed to the message of non-violence and mass organization. Bayard Rustin was arrested for allegedly having sex with men in a public place. Later we learn that the FBI had evidence that King was having extramarital affairs while leading the movement. The organizations that they founded, like the SCLC, were in crisis, but they survived. Yet we must say: "so what?" This is war, not a quest for moral righteousness. My friend Mukassa Dada stated that when King's friends and others went to confirm some of the FBI's suspicions, he said to himself: "Great, that means that he was like me!" When you are about change and you are fighting oppression, imperfect people will be the best to use in the struggle and the moral issue is not a factor! This does not mean that it is ok to be immoral, but the need for commitment to liberation makes room for the individual proclivities of those who are struggling for freedom. One of Malcom X's major issues, as told by some who followed him, was that he required what his followers characterized as an extreme form of moral observance: no alcohol, no women, no reefer, no cursing. He taught the strict teaching of Islam in his organization Muslim Mosque Inc. Yet when Malcolm observed that the most dedicated to his "cause" were hung up in some of the stuff he was involved in when he was Malcom Little, he formed another organization with the help of Dr. John Henrick Clarke and others in Harlem: the Organization of Afro-American Unity (OAAU), which followed the ethos of the Organization of African Unity (OAU) established in 1963 in Addis Abba Ethiopia. The OAAU would consist of those brothers who did not wish to follow the tenants of Islam but were fully committed to the cause of liberation. A person does not have to be pure in his flesh to lead a community or be a foot soldier, yet he or she is required to have sincere motives and a clear conscience.

> "True leadership demands complete subjugation of self, absolute honesty, integrity and uprightness of character, courage and fearlessness and above all a consuming love for one's people."
> Robert Sobukwe

The purpose of this presentation is to assist in the formation of effective community organization. While we are not looking to start new groups, we ate hoping to provide techniques on how to increase effectiveness of those already in existence. Community organization is not long term, but it focused on dealing with issues, problems and objectives. Community organizing is about purpose, not personality. It's about plans, not any one individual person. This is important because community organizations tend to be extensions of the egos of the people who started the organization. This means that the group is subject to the whims of its founder, and not on sound teaching and clear vision. Most efforts at effective community organizing live and die as issues emerge and disappear; as problems rise and fall; and as opportunities present themselves or are lost. Just because an organization is successful in one time period does not mean that they will be successful in the next unless the organization is willing to change along with the demands of the season. Sometimes, the success of the efforts leads to its demise and sometimes issues become moot or lose their appeal.

Outside Agitators Are the Most Effective

It is arrogant to come, as many altruistic do-gooders do, into a ghetto and free the savage and backwards black people into civility. Every year, ghettos see hundreds of "inner city" workers come into the ghetto with the expectation of lifting the veil of ignorance on the little Negro people only to leave with tears in their eyes. This is a form of arrogant localized colonialism. Outsiders cannot help a community until the community has organized to receive them, which means there must be a change of consciousness and an internal dynamism created by those people before they can be organized from without. So the community organizer must strategically target certain demographics that are on the verge of change from within. To be an effective organizer, one must be commissioned by the community to come into their community space and rearrange things in a way that puts power in the hands of the people. Only an organized people can have power, and this organization must be intentional and not reactionary. Meaning that waiting on the cops to kill a black man will never bring anything but chaos, confusion and violence. Yet an organized initiative sparks an entirely different involvement which put loud mouths and busy bodies to the back. The organizer makes statements and offers assistance and starts with a small group. However, he or she only advocates ideas not action. All action is agreed upon by the community because it is they who will have to live with the consequences. Over time the community begins to trust the organizer. Until then, he is an alien, a visitor, an outsider and outside agitator and it is good that he remain so. The need for the organizer must precede his call, meaning the people will have already expressed concern over an issue that is getting worse over time—which could include intolerance for the status quo. The purpose of organizing is to obtain power but this cannot be done without the shifting of power away from those who currently possess it. The organizer—as an outsider—understands power because he or she comes from it and serves as an ambassador to the powerless. Jesus Christ kept reminding the people that He was not from earth and would not remain here long. "I came from God" before delivering a message that could be summarized as" look you stupid people, I am come from heaven and being in this body is getting old, you want a new body that does not leak, stink, or die come with me," and, this is a big, "or else."

Or Else!

Because the hegemony within the local power structure—both white and black—will not instinctively give it up, these same people have to be faced with consequences for not giving in to the demands of the community. This is what we call the "or else" factor. Most black people have been conditioned to negotiate or bargain from a position of weakness or altruism. Altruism is an appeal to the weaknesses of human beings, which means that when black people do beg the city for something, the assumption is that black people are the only benefactor and the relationship is benevolent and not contractual. When a community recognizes power, it is able to make threats and ultimatums come to pass if the demands are not made properly. The community organizer must very quickly begin to put the group in a position to make threats and back those threats up with action, which is direct and positive. The term positive action is used by President Kwame Nkrumah who applied political party politics to overcome the colonial powers which had controlled Ghana for years. Positive action was non-violent but very aggressive to the point that the tenet was questionable.

However, the protests, marches, boycotts and demonstrations worked to weaken the political hegemony in Ghana. All effective community organizing focuses on placing political power in the hands of the citizens most affected by the problems and not those distant from the problems. No one can tell the group what should be important nor can someone else prescribe the remedy. Community organizing organically grows out of the rights guaranteed in the U.S. Constitution. Frederick Douglass stated *"Power concedes nothing without demand"* and it is the demand of the people which gets thing done in a republic. Power in the hands of the injured or marginalized makes the bastions of power very nervous, but makes the self-determination of the people possible. The aim of progress for the community is to have the ideas and pursuits of the community materialize in the form desired by the group. A community does not need others to tell them what is good for them or to convince them that something is better than something else. Instead, a community tells those in positions to do their job or get fired! The resistance to community organizing is the same all over. Distractions, delays and bureaucracy are all seen as roadblocks to progress, but the folks at the city will tell the groug that *"progress"* is being made and that *"relationships"* have been built, which typically are code words for non-action. A community organization must be selfish, stubborn, and hostile to any excuse that prevents it from getting what it wants. There is nothing more fulfilling than to see one's desires manifest as a result of his or her own efforts, and to be respected by those pinheads downtown! "Hello Mr. Johnson, Hello Mrs. Jones, thank you for your help in getting that new playground or the erection of that new community center." Yet under their breath, they are saying: "I hate that b'tch and that n#gger makes me sick!" A mayor must understand that the community organization will take the full credit for whatever positive comes from their actions, but he or she will only get a photo and his or job out of the deal! You know you have arrived when you are not invited to meetings, excluded from parties and public events but are asked when you show up: "What are you doing here?"

The next few pages will be devoted to community organizations that made a difference in their local communities that resulted in sweeping changes throughout the country and the world.

CHAPTER 4
Profiles of Community Organization

1865 From Marion to Montgomery

1955: The Montgomery Improvement Association and The Women's Political Council v. The City of Montgomery and the U.S. Automakers

A community organizer must distinguish between material and symbolic victories. After the Montgomery Bus Boycott, the U.S. Department of Transportation, the Alabama Department of Transportation and the big wigs from the American Auto Industry got together to create a major extension of Alabama's interstate system, which would run bull dozers right through the black community. Ask anybody during that time and they will say that the black community was self-sufficient to the point that many blacks did not experience much racial mistreatment except in common areas like the bus system. There were black movie theaters, black restaurants, black drug stores, black medical facilities, black shoe stores, and other businesses. Yet all of this was threatened by newly formulated interstate plans which could not be stopped. The black citizens of Montgomery were called to community meetings and tried to organize around those meetings to prevent the plans of this multifaceted group to run Interstate 85 and the Interstate 65 Interchange through the heart of Montgomery's black economic district—thus destroying their housing value and decimating the local economy. This was not limited to Montgomery—it was the master plan throughout the country. They knew that the issue of the day was no longer integration, but rather, mobilization. An observation Martin Luther

King would express in his book *Where Do We Go From Here: Chaos Or Community?* Notice the statistics for Montgomery and black belt which shows an upward trajectory of income growth in Montgomery after the boycott even though we can conclude that the political power has not increased.

TABLE 2. Percentage of Population Below Poverty Line in Back Belt Counties in Alabama

		1959-1960	1969-1970	1979-1980	1989-1990	1999-2000	2009-2013
1	Barbour	65.65	43.7	30.81	25.02	26.08	26.7
2	Bullock	72.23	54.9	35.45	36.5	33.5	21.6
3	Butler	63.27	42.1	27.16	31.5	24.6	28.4
4	Dallas	58.53	40.20	32.29	35.5	31.1	35.05
5	Choctaw	62.11	42.1	31.47	30.2	24.5	21.1
6	Crenshaw	65.18	45.4	29.82	24.3	22.1	19.1
7	Greene	78.15	65.5	45.67	45.6	34.1	32.9
8	Hale	72.29	54.9	39.52	35.6	19.1	26.6
9	Lowndes	77.81	61.8	44.99	38.6	31.1	26.7
10	Macon	61	46.5	32.98	34.5	32.8	27.3
11	Marengo	63.62	46.4	33.38	30	25.9	24.1
12	Montgomery	36.62	25.1	19.4	17.9	17.3	21.2
13	Perry	76	47.5	43.78	42.6	35.4	25.6
14	Pike	62.27	38.9	27.37	27.2	23.1	27.6
15	Russell	50.2	35.3	24.72	20.4	19.9	22.0
16	Sumter	74.08	53.1	33.65	39.7	38.7	38.9
17	Wilcox	78.93	56.8	45.28	45.2	39.9	39.2

Source: Census 1960, 1970, 1980, 1990, 2000; American Community Survey, 2013

Although the chart above shows an increase in wages, it does not show an increase in the ability to advance life, liberty and the pursuit of happiness.

After the plans were announced, meetings were held in the black community and very heated discussions took place. Yet the victory of the boycott was unable to transition into advancement. It was not long before the earthmoving machines began to fire up and the homes, businesses and abodes of black people were reduced to ashes. What we have discovered by using GIS technology is that the Interstate at the place of Jackson Hospital and Forrest Avenue makes an unusual curve to the north which cannot be explained except that the surveyors intentionally ran the highway into the black community rather than divert away from it. Interestingly enough the black community also did not have an exit and entrance to the corridor which prevented traffic from coming into and out of the black community. All traffic would be steered away from the black community and toward downtown. All of this was by design. If this is not systemic racism, I don't know what is? Notice in the GIS provided by myself and Dr. Ram Alagan.

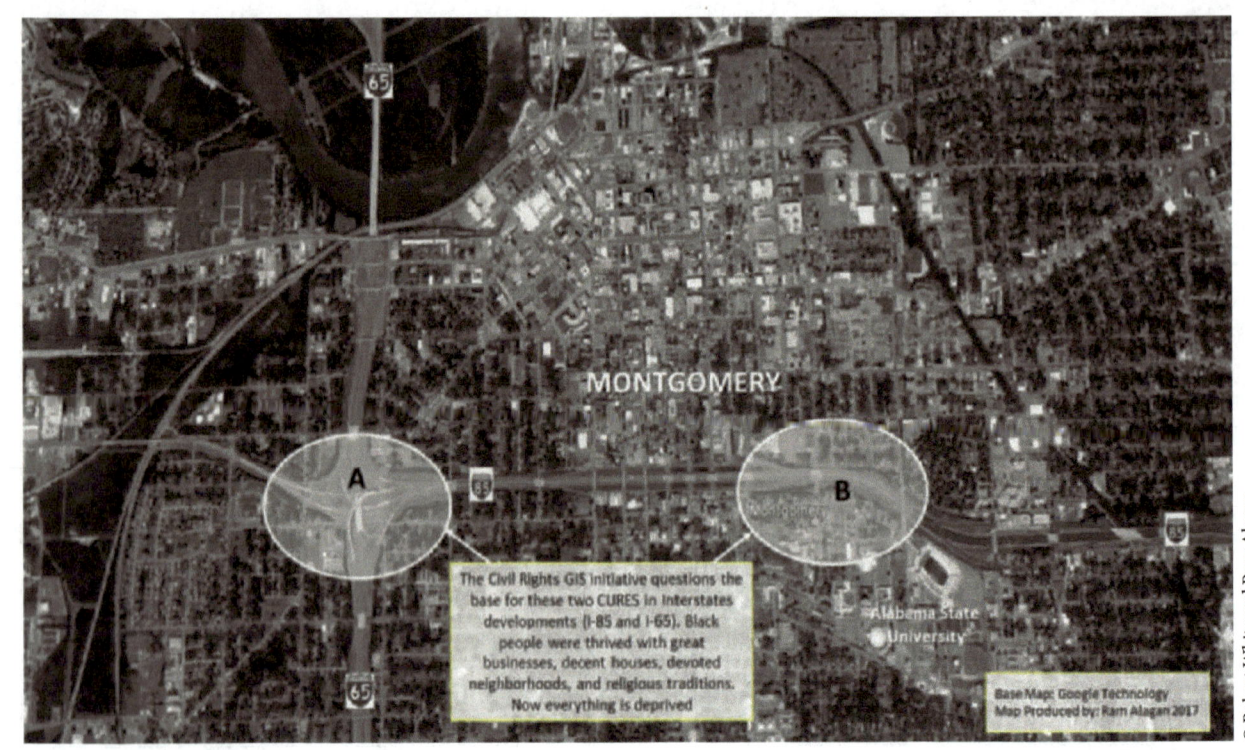

> The Civil Rights GIS Initiative questions the base for these two CURES in Interstates developments (I-85 and I-65). Black people were thrived with great businesses, decent houses, devoted neighborhoods, and religious traditions. Now everything is deprived

Black people also saw their parks and pools close and they seemed powerless to defeat it. What caused such a defeat after the success of the boycott? Some erroneously assume that the black community collapsed because those Negroes with cars moved away to white communities when there is little hard evidence to support this assertion. During the boycott--though not because of it—the entire dynamics of the nation's cities changed to generally requiring a commute longer than 5 miles. This made automobile usage preferable and necessary. Soon, car ownership became a status thing even among the black middle class. Also, for reasons we will discuss later, the black community did not have the means of mobilization after the buses shut down and they became isolated from the jobs and opportunities that were once available to them. During the boycott, the lack of black maids in the homes of white people struck a major cord with the southern lifestyle and placed every white household in danger of dissolution because of the need of the Negro woman. This dynamic worked against the black community after the boycott. Rather than use the boycott as a means to divorce themselves from their dependency on public transportation—which would have been the creation of what is now Uber or Lift—blacks tried to resume their old ways which became their undoing. The rest of the world changed on a dime and black people could not adapt to the change. Some community organizers are under a false assumption that the black community has suffered because those most moral around them were those professionals who also had the means to leave the community.

CHAPTER 4: Profiles of Community Organization

I-85 and I-65 Impacts to Local Communities

© Robert White

I-65 and I-85 Intersection in Montgomery

© Robert White

I-65 and I-85 Intersection in Montgomery

A Display Local Community for I-85 and I-65 and Its Impacts to Local Community

© Robert White

© Robert White

Abandoned Homes in the Vicinity of I-85 and I-65

The "Or Else!" Factor

This could not be the further from the truth because the evidence does not show this! In fact, according to E. Franklin Frazier, the black bourgeoise class was the least resistant to the status quo created by Jim Crow, having benefited from the very system that the black masses were trying to undo or reform. Instead, the black community allowed itself to be reorganized by the same powers that did so during segregation and its leaders emerged as the new enforcers of the old system. What is wrong with black leadership in Montgomery is that it emerged from a time when the old status quo was the order of the day. That is why the biggest hindrance to black power and advancement is black leadership. Even now, most of the black businesses are still in the hood, suffering from the same conditions as they did in the 50s. Also property ownership remains the same. But what is lacking is the growth necessary to support expansion.

1960: Gomillion v. Lightfoot: From A Square to A 28 Sided Polygon

To accompany judicial action, the locals under the leadership of a Tuskegee Institute professor Charles Gomillion and others under the guise of the Tuskegee Civic Association, staged a boycott of local businesses, which had the same galvanizing and mobilizing effect among African Americans of different backgrounds as it did in Montgomery[1]. Prior to the passage of Act 140 by the state legislature, which disfranchised virtually all of its black residents, the boundary of the city was a square. However, after Act 140 was passed by the state legislature, the shape of the city's boundary changed to a 28 sided polygon. Such an act that would be considered by the court "tantamount for all practical purposes to a mathematical demonstration, that the legislation is solely concerned with segregating white and colored voters by fencing Negro citizens out of town so as to deprive them of their pre-existing municipal vote[2]." After a ruling from the District Court stating that the state did act within their rights in drawing the voting districts and after that ruling was upheld by the Appellate Court, the attorneys for the appellate (which included Fred Gray of Browder v. Gayle fame, Charles Carter and Author Shores) filed to have the case reviewed. In 1960, the U.S. Supreme Court held that the city's proposal to draw voting boundaries (known as gerrymandering) while not unconstitutional on its face[3], did violate the 14th Amendment rights of the city's black citizens and the previous map was reinstated. While the issue of the division of power between the federal government and that of the states remains the typical prevailing legal question when dealing with civil rights, the diminished means to accomplish ends that the court considers unconstitutional remains commonplace. Yet the issues of unconstitutional gerrymandering continue to be a means of disfranchisement in the south. It would be this local battle over boundary lines, along with other similar cases, that would give momentum for the national push to modify existing laws protecting the right of Negroes to vote. Ask the citizens of Tuskegee of the lengths people will go through to disfranchise people from making decisions that impact them.

---

1. Allen Mendenhall, "Gomillion v. Lightfoot", Encyclopedia of Alabama, 2011/2014
2. Gomillion v. Lightfoot, 364 U.S. 339 (1960)
3. United States v. Reading Co., 226 U. S. 324, 226 U. S. 357

FIGURE-3: Civil Rights vs. Geo-informatics Technology

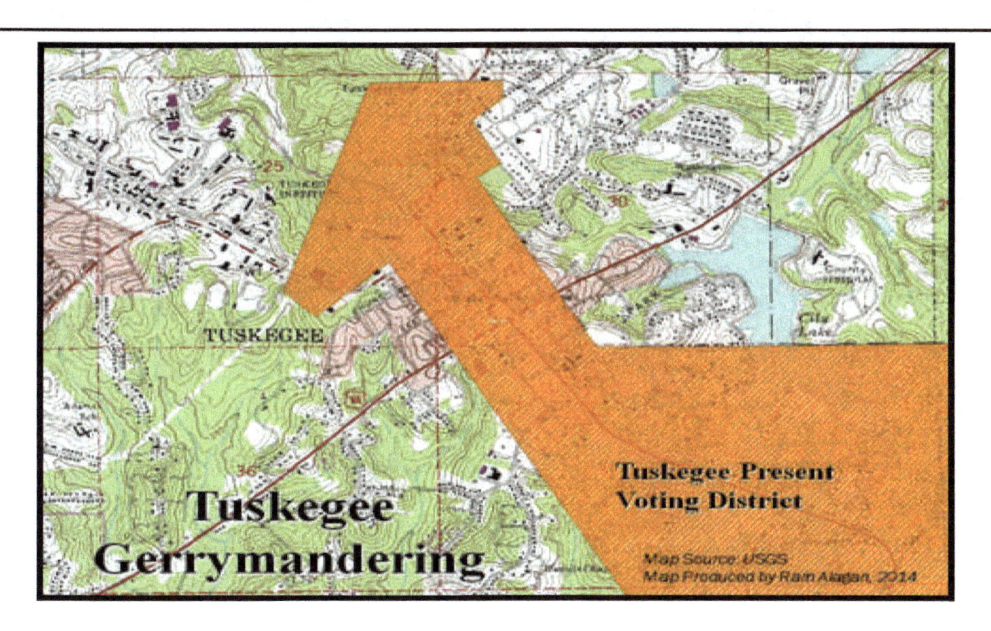

Voting District Gerrymandering in Tuskegee,
Alabama Vs. Geo-informatics Technology
(Source: Ram Alagan, 2013)

1965: SNCC, SCLC and The Selma to Montgomery March

The death of Jimmy Lee Jackson in Marion, Alabama served to spark a campaign which climaxed with a march from Selma to Montgomery. Although the first objective of the march, to bring attention to the death of the local fallen comrade in arms diminished and the need for national attention to voting rights emerged as a greater priority, the movement started there began to take on a different character than the grassroots efforts which had been sustained but unsuccessful up unto that point. The Black belt was the hot bed for voting rights activity; the region being selected by the Student Non-Violent Coordinating Committee (SNCC) as good place to test the strength of the Jim Crow system of voter suppression. SNCC was organized by Ella Baker to be the grunt workers for the preachers who seemed less apt to community organize. The result of the grassroots efforts in Lowndes County Alabama, which spun from their efforts in Greensboro, Mississippi months prior, would result in the birth of organizations like the Lowndes County Freedom Organization, the Black Panther Party for Self Defense and others. Also, in Dallas county, the Dallas County Voter's League led by F.D. Reese and others set the stage for King's appearance. Dallas County became the point of confrontation between massive resistance efforts and law enforcement and with the intense violence of local and state law enforcement officials served to bring enough international attention to the plight of the Negroes living there to bring about legislation in the form of the Voting Rights Act. In the past, black voters were subject to literacy tests, poll taxes, intimidation and lynching; all for the purpose of suppressing the black vote.

CHAPTER 5
The Games People Play

ENVISION 20/20

As stated in this book, the civil rights movement had about as much to do with changing economic conditions such as white flight and redlining than with segregation. As city demographics changed, immobile blacks found themselves unable to get to where the jobs were located. Those in power love to keep the people from reacting to their agenda and what better way to defuse a revolt or insurrection than to promise the people that progress or freedom is imminent. Slavery was only supposed to last 70 years but instead endured 400 years and it took a bloody civil war to end it. This is because the slaves kept believing the master's promises that they would be free very soon! The master would build the slaves up for a gradual let down, casting them deeper into psychological slavery with each promise to the point that, according to Harriet Jacobs, slave masters could not be trusted no matter how convincing they may sound. The most effective technique of the power elite is to energize or inflate the people's hopes and then slowly zap the energy and momentum out of people—thus frustrating them. This is called *energizing*. Energizing serves many purposes. One, it identifies those in the community who are interested, which is to say, those people who could pose a potential problem. Usually you have to register and sign up which means they have your name, phone number and address. Energizing also serves as a means of assuring that reorganization does not happen under the pretense of change but progress. The technique is to get the people excited and expectant that things will change and to get them to invest so much intellectual capital in their hope that they cannot organize or put up a formidable obstacle to their plans.

For fear of being labelled a trouble maker or problematic, the people remain silent and watch things that they did not agree to or mention come to form before their very eyes. One historic example occurred, about 20 years ago, when a plan emerged to use Montgomery as a breadbasket for neighboring counties, which took place under the theme of "Envision 20/20." It was headed up by the Chamber of Commerce and the Mayor's Office and used trusted African American leaders as front men and women. This plan would create a tri-county or River Region whereby the City of Montgomery could be used on paper to acquisition funds to build up what would be called the Preferred Communities of Prattville, Millbrook and Wetumpka while simultaneously draining Montgomery of its appeal. Many things would happen to make this possible. Land was purchased and sold to developers, eminent domain issues emerged to literally steal land, and a public relations campaign was created to make Montgomery look as bad as possible while building up downtown Montgomery and neglecting other communities. Even now, the headlines speak of nothing but crime, violence, corruption and confusion while making things seem quiet and tranquil in the suburbs. This is done to create a housing market in Prattville—and it worked! Initially, people from Montgomery were invited to the community interest meetings, paired in inter-racial and multi-demographical groups which gave the appearance that things had changed, now blacks and whites were sitting down and talking about things. "Look blacks and whites are together, sitting down and discussing the problems and solutions!" They had the easels of paper and some attentive facilitator with a marker in hand to write the topics on the paper. You know the drill…they would take down all the suggestions and feedback, elect a table spokesperson, and then have this big follow up session to reveal the groups input. However, community organizers do not need input because they have been commissioned to address the obvious! After these events ended, the invitees seemed to be satisfied that things were looking up. Yet this was a façade. The meetings became more scarce and the promise to resume the meetings was abandoned. The energetic and eager group who thought they were being the change were actually fodder for a skilled public relations firm whose only job was to fulfill a grant requirement to have public hearings. Soon Montgomery would see its resources drained, its population headed down the Highway 31 and its major community partner Maxwell Airforce Base withdraw its support from the very community it had sworn to build up. We would soon enter wars with foreign nations and after destroying them, pledge more money to rebuild them than they pledged to invest in West Montgomery. Right now, Montgomery is like a nursing mother to Prattville, Millbrook, Wetumka and Pike Road who serve as spoiled and entitled brats that consume every drop of milk from its mother's depleting black breasts. Sadly, they see no need to replenish her. Montgomery gives and gives and they take, take, take, take and all of this was signed, sealed and delivered with thunderous applause from ignorant Montgomerians under the false flag of change and community involvement! When a mayor with some courage comes to the office and threatens to end the looting of Montgomery, he is sent to the principal's office, which is a legislature controlled by former slave masters who refuse to give black municipalities autonomy and home rule. This is the parasitic and exploitative nature of the tri-county area and it is against this which we seek to organize.

Sometimes separate groups form independent of each other and attempt to merge. However, sometimes remaining unified in purpose while being separate in identity is a good strategy. The scope of community organizing is very limited and sometimes forming a united front gives a better appearance than having one organization. If others from outside the immediate community join in the purpose and it begins to spread throughout the city, state and then nation, it comes to a mass emphasis. But until then, a community organization should focus on its immediate tasks. Because all politics are local, the most effective community organizations understand and seek to master local political power first and leave the statewide and national movements to other people. However, local organizations must be careful not to be organized from without—meaning by people outside the community. Taking money from outside organizations bind the local organization to the agenda of some party that might not be in sync with the group's ethos. For example, some local organizations are promised money if they wear certain organizations t-shirts and show up for their events but this is confusing to the people because it is never clear who is running the show. Blurring the line is a deal breaker because local organizations are built from the integrity of the local people and not an outside group. It has been said that it is harder to organize a community than it is to organize a nation. It is for this reason that city hall becomes a bigger battle ground than Capitol Hill. Yet sometime local action leads you straight to the national scene—especially if the issue is media sensitive. Such was the case with the Mississippi Freedom party. Community organizers must understand that their arch enemy and their biggest ally is the mayor. So all local organizations should be mentally prepared to have a love/hate relationship and betray it whenever is necessary. The reader should do research on the power of mayors like Joseph Smitherman in Selma, Richard Dailey in Chicago, Johnny Ford in Tuskegee, Rudy Guliani in New York, Manard Jackson in Atlanta and Emory Folmer in Montgomery.

Understanding municipal government, how it works and its weaknesses are critical to navigating the bureaucracy. Community organizing circumvents the tangle of pathology that mayors and city councilpersons create to shield themselves from public scrutiny and accountability. City managers, supervisors and chiefs of staff are not the ones who will be on the receiving end of criticism, retaliation and threats. In the end, the mayor is the target and his cronies lose their ability when the community organization engages him or her directly. Community organizers should be intently and intensely taught that everything begins, ends and depends on the community organization to get their way. The community organizer sets his or her sights on the weakest aspect of the mayor's office which is typically its public relations office. However, the tactics of the group must be unassuming first. It must show that it is the best example on how to handle a situation. An excellent example of this is the now-defunct group that was called F.A.C.E (Fathers Active in Children's Education). This organization worked the community, re-organized it out of the hands of Emory Folmer's regime, and made significant change in the community while electing one of its founders to the position of city council—the late brother Willie Cook. It was Willie Cook, working with my brother-in-law, which got Montgomery the Tax-Free Holliday which started in Birmingham. Willie Cook was also fundamental in defeating the city's policy of road blocks which after obtaining an Attorney General's opinion from Bill Pryor was determined to be suspect of constitutional soundness. These are two examples of how community organizing helped shape local policy. Other organizations like WINGS and Enough is Enough are also good examples of attempts at sustained efforts. Yet the reactionary nature of the last two groups prevent them from being mentioned in the same light as FACE—although they did assist in raising community awareness. Yet the effectiveness of "getting the word out" and "community awareness" activities are almost impossible to assess.

The Ordinary People's Society

The most comprehensive example of effective community organizing was set in motion by an ex-felon who wished to be counted as a citizen. He discovered that after his term had been served that he was ineligible to vote and began a campaign to have his and other voting rights restored. His efforts would cover every aspect of effective activism, which is issue advocacy, lobbying, policy change, political action, and then legislative change. Seldom does an organization begin in the streets and conclude a process with the passage or failure of legislation. Included in the book is a copy of the legal brief and other correspondence associated with the success of the effort. When ordinary people take action, the status quo is in trouble. One of the most successful organizations in community organizing and issue advocacy was formed by Rev. Kenneth Glasgow and others to assist in the restoration of voting rights to ex-felons. I met Rev Glasgow at the Alabama State House while lobbying for the Secretary of State's office. He was in the lobby of the legislature and he was wearing a sign around his neck that said: "I am a citizen." This made him stand out and when he found out I was the interim director of elections, he and I formed a friendship. He made his way to my office and we begin to discuss the implications of an effort that was going to be one of the most significant victories of the civil rights era. Before Rev. Glasgow's and TOPS' effort would conclude, Glasgow would file a lawsuit that would be known as Glasgow v. Allen which opened the door for sweeping change in the area of felony voting, exposed the corrupt manner in which the state and political parties had been disenfranchising thousands of voters through incarceration, and championed a policy change wherein the Secretary of State sent mandates to local sheriffs and prison wardens ensuring that eligible incarcerated persons vote and gave segue to the clarification of vague legal terms like "moral turpitude." Rev. Glasgow and his fellow workers went to jails and prisons and advocated on behalf of incarcerated persons and became a very high profile voice in the world of civil rights. Although his organization has not received the credit they deserve for that ground breaking success, as one freedom fighter from Nigeria, Obi Egbuna Sr., phrased it: "You must be prepared to be ignored." The effort of TOPS also inspired the legislation of helpful acts such as *the First Step Act* and the *Fair Sentencing Act*. See Appendix

There are no friends in politics but there are many allies, alliances, caucuses and blocks. A community organizer must understand politics and not take things personally. When organizers take attacks personally, they lose their effectiveness. Organizers should always remain out of the way, even phantasmal to the point that they are indistinguishable from others among the community. The powers that be should be asking:" Which one is the leader?" Because the community organizer is not the voted upon or recognized leader, he or she has leisure to move as needed. Yet the organizer trains leadership and has trust that they will not go rogue.

The Montgomery Improvement Association

The City of Montgomery and the White Citizens Council did everything they could to stop the boycott. First, the mayor refused to hear the complaints of the citizens and then summarily dismissed the requests of the community. Then, after the boycott started, the mayor commandeered several local pastors (none of which were a part of the MIA) to falsely claim that an agreement had been reached and the bus boycott should be over. The attorney for King and Parks (Fred Gray) was spotted to be drafted in the military and the various members of all community organization were subject to house bombings, intimidations and threats. At the conclusion of the protest, the local white merchants started their own campaign to "fire yo nigga."

In January 1956, Martin Luther King was briefly jailed for driving 30 miles an hour in a 25 mile per hour zone. A month later, he was one of eighty-nine people indicted for violating Alabama's anti-boycott statute, which imposed criminal penalties for any conspiracy to interfere with the operation of any business "without a just cause or legal excuse." Both sides agreed that Dr. King would be tried first and that the other cases would be held in abeyance until his was resolved. The mass meeting was set for 7pm to take place at Holt Street Baptist Church.

Rosa Parks stated so many times that all she did was sit down. Yet she did plenty of field work that never makes it into the record. It is a sad and, in some instances, an intentional omission to not mention the efforts of others who built the bus protest effort. Joanne Robinson and Mary Fair Burke were the builders of the Women's Political Council—the organization which first began to mention economic boycotts. When denied admittance into the League of Women Voters, these women started their own organization which lead to the culmination of the bus protest. It is called a *protest* because, as Attorney Fred Gray stated, that a boycott is an illegal activity under Alabama law. E.D. Nixon considering his union organizational skills with the Union of Sleeping Car Porters also considered a boycott or strike of sorts as a necessary means of obtaining better treatment. Yet no one could really define what better treatment was all about. There was no national example from which a standard could be set. At this point, we have three organizations emerge, the local NAACP, the Women's Political Council (WPC) and the Montgomery Improvement Association (MIA) with strong influence given by Joanne Robinson, E.D. Nixon and Rufus Lewis. To understand the difference and clashes that emerged especially between Lewis and Nixon is to appreciate the intensity in which puppies play. Their argument, which could have threatened the entire operation, was about strategy—and I am told that it turned personal. However, in community organizing there should be no cult of personalities or ruling elite, only a hierarchy of ideas! People think that King came to Montgomery to lead the boycott, which is the furthest from the truth. Instead, he came to do research at Alabama Teacher's College under the oversight of Dr. Lawrence Reddick, who was then chair of the History Department at Alabama State Teachers College. The testimony of the plaintiff in the Browder v. Gayle case is critical to understanding community organizing and the phantom manner in which the organizers must operate. The attorneys for the city tried to get the plaintiff to characterize King as the "leader" of the movement. Instead, they all consistently stated that he was selected by the people to be the representative. Now, this is pure republicanism in true democratic fashion. In a republic, there are no leaders or ruling intellectual elite because every man has his own right to be his own leader. However, a republic is a representative form of government and effective community organizers don't lead people in ways they don't know, but simply organizes them to go in a direction that everyone agrees is the best way. After the Browder decision was handed down and the buses were integrated, the city terminated the bus system all together, but not for the reason that one might assume. In 1950, the State of Alabama passed an amendment that limited gas tax revenues for roads and bridges. The Alabama Department of Transportation became the most powerful arm of state government. Interstates were built which made travel easier and funds were cut for urban transportation (namely the bus systems) as the market for automobiles began to skyrocket. With the emergence of a new automobile market, the issue became mobility, not segregation. It is unscientific to say that after segregation ended all the people left the community—as if all of the morality in the black community was held by those who possessed an automobile. Instead, those who depended on public transportation could not get to the sides of town that were experiencing the growth. Many whites had already started buying their black maids cars to compensate for the changing times. However, the need for automobiles to keep the black woman in the white man's home was essential to the southern way of life! If you did not work for a white man, you had no car and were subject to fall into poverty. Proximity remains a major controlling factor in the politics of a city. How far kids live from good schools, healthy food and rising property values is a fundamental topic for community organization. If the buses were destined to be eliminated anyway, why is the boycott or protest not celebrated as a partial victory when it comes to reaching a marked objective? King did not just have a dream, but he had a plan that was spelled out in his work *Where Do We Go From Here?* He talks about strikes, community organizing and the economic factors peculiar to urban areas. King focuses specifically on the role that transportation plays in the mobilization of a work force, the relocation of blacks into more affluent neighborhoods, and the access of urban black youth to white schools. Most of your desegregation cases regarding education were closely associated with the immobility of black people, which also impacts the issue of affordable and acceptable housing!

The bus system was not run by the city but the city of course was the stockholder. The city diverted attention away from the demands of the MIA, which did not involve integration of the buses. In fact, the list of demands which was ignored by the city simply involved better treatment and the hiring of black bus drivers. Because the City Line Bus was an out state company, the city simply claimed that it had no say in what the buses did and, at trial, the Public Service Commission was called upon to give testimony—most of which had little to do with the treatment that blacks was receiving on the buses. A community organizer has to understand that the real seat of power in the case of the City Line was neither at the state capital nor in Chicago: it was downtown! The mayor, William "Tackey" Gayle, was the indirect target of a very crafty public relations campaign which sought to put pressure on him to give into the demands. By then, whites all over the south had mobilized to form White Citizens Council to maintain the status quo. Mayor Gayle found himself in the newspaper constantly and having to defend himself and his tactics only led to more confusion. He tried to create a counter group of non-aligned black preachers which backfired and he was named in the Browder v. Gayle case but was evasive in giving statements which showed his unwillingness to be directly associated with the issue although his name is represented in the style of the case. He even tried to declare the boycott over as a diversionary tactic which the people saw right through. Mayor Gayle was drug out from behind his desk and forcing the mayor to respond to King and the MIA was critical in weakening the mayor in the eyes of the people. Yet he did not recant or give in. He and others could always blame their defeat on the U.S. Supreme Court who refused to hear the city's appeal to the lower court's decision.

My daughter stated in a conversation that I had with her when she was in elementary school: "Daddy, every leader in the bus boycott had a car, including Dr. Martin Luther King!" This leads me to a major point about community organizing. The organizer is not a part of the group he seeks to organize nor is he or she a benefactor of their success. Although King, Abernathy and many of the boycotts leaders were not directly affected by the boycott nor had they suffered ill treatment on the buses, they interceded on behalf of others suffering bad treatment such as incarceration, death threats and bombings. Then, a car was symbol of status which makes the appeal of the organizer that much stronger among the people. The people will not respect an organizer who is not organized his or herself and the best organizers are those who make it clear that they have the ability to drive away at any time! It was unusual for King and others who were somewhat middle class at the time to condescend to those of low estate. Because no one could claim ownership of the boycott because it so many moving parts, King became the voice of the movement which drew people to the mass meetings to partake in a democratic process. This is "We the People" in practice!

Someone asked me the other day; "was the Rosa Parks' stand staged?" I responded: "I sure hope so. If it was staged it shows our ability to strategically organize around a weakness in the system and use a minor victory to reach mass emphasis." Mrs. Parks kept saying: "All I did was keep my seat." She had to say this because if it looked like it was deliberate the court case of Browder v. Gayle would have been doomed because the court does not grant relief for offenses which occurred during events that are staged. Rosa Parks and the four plaintiffs knew how to walk the line as should all organizers but they could not take the credit for what they did because it would jeopardize their efforts.

Bibliography

I've Got The Light of Freedom: The Organizing Tradition and the Mississippi Freedom Struggle - Charles Payne

Rules for Radicals: A Pragmatic Primer For Realistic Radicals - Saul Alinsky

Hammer and Hoe: Alabama Communist During The Great Depression - Robin DG Kelley

A History of America in Ten Strikes - Erik Loomis

Five Dollars and a Pork Chop Sandwich - Mary Frances Berry

Organized Labor and the Black Worker, 1619-1981 - Philip S. Foner

No Shortcuts: Organizing For Power In The New Gilded Age - Jane F. McAlevey

Doing Democracy: The MAP Model for Organizing Social Movements - Bill Moyers

Bloody Lowndes: Civil Rights and Black Power in Alabama's Black Belt - Hasan Kwame Jeffries

That Nonviolent Stuff'll Get You Killed: How Guns Made The Civil Rights Movement Possible - Charles E. Cobb